SACRED CONVERSATION

SACRED CONVERSATION

EXPLORING THE SEVEN GIFTS OF SPIRITUAL DIRECTION

Marsha Crockett

UPPER ROOM BOOKS®
NASHVILLE

SACRED CONVERSATION: Exploring the Seven Gifts of Spiritual Direction

Upper Room Books® website: upperroombooks.com

Scripture quotations marked (AP) are the author's paraphrase.

At the time of publication, all websites referenced in this book were valid. However, due to the fluid nature of the Internet, some addresses may have changed or the content may no longer be relevant.

Cover design: Jeff Miller, Faceout Studio
Cover imagery: Shutterstock
Interior design and typesetting: PerfecType | Nashville, TN

Library of Congress Cataloging-in-Publication Data

Names: Crockett, Marsha, 1957- author.
Title: Sacred conversation : exploring the seven gifts of spiritual direction / Marsha Crockett.
Identifiers: LCCN 2021051577 (print) | LCCN 2021051578 (ebook) | ISBN 9780835819930 (print) | ISBN 9780835819947 (epub)
Subjects: LCSH: Spiritual direction. | Spiritual life--Christianity.
Classification: LCC BV5053 .C76 2022 (print) | LCC BV5053 (ebook) | DDC 253.5/3--dc23/eng/20211208
LC record available at https://lccn.loc.gov/2021051577
LC ebook record available at https://lccn.loc.gov/2021051578

To my sister, Linda McQuinn Carlblom,
my life-long companion on this
amazing journey through life.

CONTENTS

ACKNOWLEDGMENTS

Many individuals have contributed their skill, support, time, and encouragement to me during my work on this project. In the most literal sense, you would not be reading this book if it were not for the efforts and partnership of the following people.

My one and only sister, Linda Carlblom, to whom this book is dedicated. She was my first reader and greatest cheerleader. She not only helped me envision it but allowed the words to speak to her as a representative of the target audience. My friend Kim DeBeus, CSD, was a valuable contributor in helping to refine some of my thoughts and concepts and to challenge my thinking about formation and transformation. Thank you.

The editorial team at Upper Room Books, especially the editorial director, Joanna Bradley Kennedy, who first saw the possibility of a great partnership in this project. Thank you for opening the door and graciously walking me through the process. And to Michael Stephens, my editor, who used eyes and heart to edit and bring clarity, cohesion, and grace to areas that needed a second look. Thank you.

I also must thank those women who have been my spiritual companions through the years, serving as my spiritual directors through every season of life: Carol Travilla, Sharon Taszarek,

Amanda Peterson, Terry Tripp, and Mary Hartrich. The gifts I have discovered through your presence to me are outlined in these chapters and are a direct result of your generous spirits of hospitable companionship. Thank you.

My faith community, Port Orchard United Methodist Church, beginning with Pastor Shirley DeLarme, who opened the door to the possibility of "doing something different" through small listening groups. Two groups were willing to spend eight weeks with me opening each of the gifts in this book and helping me refine the way individuals might interact with the material. Donna, Julie, and Phyllis, thank you for taking the risk to join me in listening to the movement of the Spirit at work in your world. And Curt, George, Lane, Shamus, and Terry, brave souls who were willing to step into a new model of listening and learning on the spiritual journey. Thank you.

Finally, to my husband, Ernesto, you've kept me grounded as we have learned to share life during a most unusual season of sheltering in place and working from home. You never fail to bring joy, laughter, and love into my life even during the most challenging days, and I love you for that. Thank you for your faithful companionship through it all.

INTRODUCTION

Since you've picked up this book you likely are curious about a few things. You may have heard about spiritual direction and want to know what it's all about. Or you may be wondering about your own spiritual journey and the shifts you have experienced in your faith. You may be wondering if you are the only one experiencing these changes or if everyone deals with this kind of shift. And what do you do with these realities? Is there someone to talk with about any of it, or does everyone just figure this stuff out on their own?

No one should be left alone on the journey through life, especially on the journey we call "spiritual." We are created to connect, to know others and to be known. Be assured, you are not alone even when the path feels lonely. Many fellow pilgrims walk with you. Some are living, breathing people you already know, hold dear, and may turn to for support. Other pilgrims have gone before you throughout the centuries; their voices resonate through the lives they've lived and the writings they have left as their faith legacy. And there are fellow journey-ers who are specifically called to travel this path with others—not to tell you how to walk but to walk alongside you as observers, encouragers, and people of prayer. They are known as spiritual directors or spiritual companions.

In these pages you will learn more about what spiritual direction is and what it isn't. You will explore some of the practices that have for centuries aided pilgrims in drawing closer to Jesus. But above all, beyond any new information, you will be invited to experience the possibility of transformation as you stop to ponder the gifts that are offered by the grace of God to us all. Take your time. Go slow. But if you are hungry for this content and want to rush through the reading in a hurry, do so but then take time to return to the slow work of transformation as you open your heart, mind, body, and soul to the ongoing work of God within.

You will see that my perspective is from the Christian tradition, but I have written with the hope that all who read this book will be comfortable with the language, regardless of where their faith experiences have led them. The seven gifts I identify are based purely on my own experiences and reflections in working with my own spiritual director and working as a spiritual director. References in this book to individuals are based on true interactions; however, details have been changed to protect their identities and the privacy of these holy conversations. As you work through the seven gifts presented here, be open to the limitless number of gifts available to you, perfectly suited to your own journey as you work with a spiritual director.

THE GIFT OF A SPIRITUAL DIRECTOR

Spiritual direction is a gift. But before unwrapping that gift, it's important to know what a spiritual director is not.

A director is not a therapist. A therapist or counselor is academically and clinically trained to help a client solve a problem, work through a challenge, or deal with difficulties in life by looking at underlying root causes. As clients engage in understanding the complex elements of the issues, they may grow in their understanding and ability to deal with problems in a new way, ultimately leading to resolution and typically ending the need for therapy. In therapy, a client looks for solutions and resolution to move past the need for therapy.

A spiritual director may help a directee look at these same challenges and even work together with a therapist. Yet the director partners with the directee to focus solely on how and where God is meeting them or inviting them to explore and deepen their understanding of themselves. Most directors will rarely answer the question that new directees often pose: "What do you think I should do?" The director will, however, help them search for the path within. Their job is not to say what directees should do but rather to help them learn to listen and trust their own experience with the voice of God. Spiritual direction is a never-ending journey in which a directee looks for God amid their challenges and their everyday life.

A director is not a coach. A coach helps with setting goals or achieving success in a certain area of life. One may bring these topics into a conversation with a director, but the journey of faith cannot be measured by goals or achieved through a set program. As Henri Nouwen said, "We become aware that our identity does not depend on what we have accomplished or possess, that our productivity does not define us, and that our worth is not the same as our usefulness."[1] The spiritual life is not a measurable, achievable project but rather a gift given by God or a mystery explored with God's leading.

A director isn't your best friend. This is not the person to invite to your family birthday parties or to join you on your next shopping trip. To keep the lines clear that best respect your journey, it is important that your paths not cross in more than one role. Keeping the spiritual direction relationship defined this way gives the directee the benefit of an unbiased companion not interconnected with family, friends, workplace, or small groups. The director will consistently pray for you and hold in sacred confidence all that you share of your life.

A director is a skilled and trained listener with an ear toward where you are walking on your path and an eye toward the landscape of the soul. The gifts given and received in spiritual direction flow from the heart of God through the Spirit, the ultimate spiritual director who opens those gifts to any who are willing to receive them.

The seven gifts identified in this book are foundational to spiritual experiences in many faith traditions. Yet they are offered to all as unique gifts and represent my personal experience of being in spiritual direction. These gifts are by no means the only gifts you will receive. As you enter your own experience of spiritual direction, search out and explore the gifts or blessings intended only for your journey. The following are the gifts we will explore here:

- *The Gift of Awakening*: The Divine One is giving you signs of new life and awakening in your spirit. Spiritual direction attends to those signs and awakens you to ever more awakening. What are some of the signs of waking in your life?
- *The Gift of Hospitality*: Feeling unconditionally and lavishly welcomed into the spiritual direction space and conversation provides the freedom to receive all the other gifts. What would it mean to show hospitality to your own soul?
- *The Gift of Story*: Every life is a story, held within the greatest story of the Divine One dwelling within our human experience. Intentionally looking at your life and learning to welcome the ups and downs leads to new understandings of how God's grace has always been present. What are the common themes running through your story?
- *The Gift of Pilgrimage*: Like the gift of story, pilgrimage allows us to tend to the day-to-day journey through life. We explore the landscape of the soul and find new paths to wander or shelters in which to stop and rest. What does your landscape or pathway look like in this season of life?
- *The Gift of Silence and Stillness*: Meeting with a director is the practice of pausing in our hurried, noisy lives.

Silence and stillness are about more yielding and less resisting. How are you listening to the silence?

- *The Gift of Meditation*: Jesus asked hard questions that required his listeners to meditate on his words. *Why are you afraid? Who do you say that I am? Where is your faith? What do you want?* What are the deeper questions of faith that you are sitting with?
- *The Gift of Belonging*: A contemplative life is not meant to be lived alone. Along the way we gather companions, fellow pilgrims, a "great cloud of witnesses" who journey with us and speak words of life to us. Ultimately, the contemplative life calls us outward toward a place of belonging. Where is life calling you to expand your reach, and how do you discern that calling?

I'm honored to walk with you through these pages. As you wonder and wander, look to that Divine Spirit, the true director of your soul who asks the deep questions, allows you to discover your own wisdom, and delights in holding the space for your sacred conversations.

—Marsha Crockett, 2021

one

The Gift of Awakening

Awaken your spirit to adventure;
Hold nothing back, learn to find ease in risk;
Soon you will be home in a new rhythm,
For your soul senses the world that awaits you.
—John O'Donohue, *To Bless the Space Between Us*

Sometime in the late eighties I came across two words—*spiritual direction*—that would change the trajectory of my faith journey. Although I can't recall the book or even the context, something about what I read captured my heart and mind and felt as much like a calling as anything I had ever experienced. As frequently happens when we encounter awakening, I began noticing references to spiritual direction all around me.

This led me to learn about others throughout the centuries who were well acquainted with this discipline: Julian of Norwich, Teresa of Ávila, Francis de Sales, Thomas Merton, Henri

Nouwen, Mother Teresa, and many others. Ancient mystics to modern voices showed that spiritual direction was nothing new but rather something old being rediscovered, reimagined, and reaffirmed in today's faith communities.

A common thread of understanding and practice connected these fellow pilgrims. All of them found spiritual direction to be a gift beyond measure in tending to the ever-present and ongoing movement of God in the ordinary aspects of daily life. I couldn't agree more. While I ultimately became a spiritual director myself, I first entered this practice as a directee and began meeting for one hour once a month with a woman who ended up companioning me on my journey for nearly five years, walking with me through some of my darkest days, faithfully lighting the torch that allowed me to take another step forward.

Since then, I've continued to meet monthly with a spiritual director. I've had several different ones over the years, and each has uniquely met me on the path and allowed me to dwell more deeply in the love of God as I've learned to know myself through the God who dwells within me. This book is an invitation to new directees or those curious about spiritual direction to befriend their longings or their awakenings to something more intentional and personal in their relationship with God.

The gifts offered through direction have become my personal "rule of life" (more about that in a later chapter). These gifts are my north star; they define my priorities not only in a spiritual direction relationship but also in how I choose to live every aspect of my life. They have become a template to examine my life, to realign or release what does not fit, and to embrace all that fulfills the call.

You might think spiritual direction squeezes you into a set method and means of knowing God, but in fact it does quite the opposite and offers enormous variety and potential for creative expression for both the director and the directee. Through spiritual direction, you will ultimately find your own north star defined by other unique gifts as you experience what the ancients call "tending the holy." As the psalmist says, "The boundary lines have fallen for me in pleasant places. . . . He brought me out into a broad place" (Ps. 16:6; 18:19). Along the way, you will have the opportunity to pause and reflect, to sit in silence creating space for God to direct your thoughts, to heal a hurt, or to reveal a truth.

The following chapters offer many contemplative practices as tools to open your heart to God. Don't feel overwhelmed by them or that you must practice them all. Use them to experiment and explore your relationship with God and the landscape of your soul as you feel led.

SIGNS OF WAKING

While I was discovering spiritual direction in the mid-eighties, I stumbled across Richard Foster's now classic *Celebration of Discipline*. It gave me a language for what I was experiencing spiritually but had never named. It was an awakening to the contemplative practices that had been feeding my soul, although I had never read about these practices in this depth. Whether it's a book, conversation, sermon, or an observation of the world at work, God is constantly tapping our shoulders, asking us to wake up to the divine messages in all of creation that are waiting to be received by any who have eyes to see and ears to hear.

Waking doesn't mean we are suddenly perfected, whole, or finally "getting it right." Waking is only the beginning. A light has dawned, and there's nothing to do but get up and begin to explore this new landscape. Waking also doesn't mean that life is much better now that the light allows us to see the path. It may be a relief when the light first shines, but it often shows us that we have been sleeping in a mess that we suddenly want to sort out, clean up, or leave completely.

Just as surely as we see signs when seasons change, so God gives us signs of new life or awakenings in our spirit. Here are some common factors that may suggest a readiness for entering sacred conversations with a spiritual director as you explore your journey and take notice of how you are waking up:

- A sense of wondering or questioning of faith
- A confusion about changing attitudes or circumstances that leave you feeling lost or displaced or out of sync in some way
- A feeling of being stuck, having hit an obstacle or blockade in your life
- A sense that the traditional ways and practices of knowing God are no longer working
- A shift in your understanding of God
- A desire to grow deeper in love with God or desire to have a richer life of prayer
- A loss, great or small, that stays with you and asks for your attention

- An encounter with the Divine that has opened new insights or a sense of calling
- A dryness or complacency about life in general or the spiritual journey in particular
- A transition in any area of life (a move, job change, empty nest, divorce, death) that calls for discernment of your next steps forward

These and dozens of other examples give clues that God is not only present but also longing to be known by anyone willing to join in this journey. Such seasons of change are rarely comfortable. Dismantling, rearranging, renovating, demolishing, and re-constructing are all signs of a creative process. But be assured that the creative process in the hands of a loving God—no matter how uncomfortable or disorienting—is reason for hope.

DISCOVERY AND EXPLORATION

In addition to the signs of awakening noted above, the following will help to shine a light on the areas that are emerging within you as you begin the discovery process.

Way Opening. Rather than searching for what's new (which sometimes feels like an intimidating blank canvas), consider what is passing or changing. Parker Palmer notes that the Quaker discernment tradition says, "Way will open."During one season of discernment in his life he said, "Way may open for other people, but it sure isn't opening for me."[1] But a wise friend advised that "way" may not ever open, but a lot of "way" closes behind us and has the same effect of guiding us forward toward our awakenings. What is closing behind you? What long-held habits or traditions are no longer life-giving? If you imagine life without those traditions, what new paths might open to you?

Exploration. Part of experiencing and embracing awakenings involves exploration and curiosity. What things are you wondering about lately? Where do you want to experience adventure? Or does fear of attempting something new keep nagging at you? Fear holds the potential seed of awakening. Address fear with grace. Refrain from acting for a while to give the seed a place to grow. What is it telling you and asking of you? How might you offer that seed as a prayer?

You may be thinking, *I don't have any big issues or areas of awakening going on in my life right now. Maybe I don't need a spiritual director.* Having issues to work out is not a prerequisite for being in spiritual direction. In fact, I do not have a big problem to talk about in most of my own meetings with a director. It's in my ordinary day—especially in my work life, home and family relationships, and my church community—where I'm looking for God's presence and need a companion to help me unravel and reveal where God is leading. Part of the joy of direction is knowing that someone is walking with me during my fallow seasons and planting seasons, as well as in my seasons of harvest.

God gives us the desire to know God as we come to know ourselves. As we wade through the shallows of mundane routines, we may recognize a faint but real yearning of "deep calling to deep," an awakening to ourselves and to the Divine within as we navigate life transitions, losses, new perspectives, or callings. Saint Augustine's prayer expresses this desire: "Grant, Lord, that I may know myself that I may know thee."[2] But truly knowing ourselves takes equal portions of courageous exploration, grace, and a vulnerable willingness to unravel the mystery that makes us who we are. And it requires the support of others who walk alongside us as we take that inward journey.

Sacred Conversation is an invitation to explore the contemplative practices to awaken us to that still small voice whispering within. It pulls back that shroud of mystery by exploring the gifts that enrich our lives as we become companions on the journey and dwell deep in the grace of God.

SACRED CONVERSATION

- Underline the words or phrases in this chapter that best describe your own awakening experiences. What attracts you to sharing your journey with a companion? What frightens you about this possibility?
- What are some of the clues waking in your life? How have you responded to those awakenings? If you don't feel you've experienced awakening, consider the list of clues to awakening. Which one resonates with you today?
- Of the seven gifts highlighted in this book, which are you most eager to explore or receive? What awakened you to this longing?
- How have you been supported by or engaged with others in the deeper examination of your soul? What other kinds of support would be helpful on this journey?
- What gift or grace do you most need from God to embark on this journey?

two

The Gift of Hospitality

The paradox of hospitality is that it wants to create emptiness, not a fearful emptiness, but a friendly emptiness where strangers can enter and discover themselves as created free; free to sing their own songs, speak their own languages, dance their own dances; free also to leave and follow their own vocations.

—Henri J. M. Nouwen, *Reaching Out*

I'm an introvert. I prefer a party of one to a party of fifty. I'm filled up, calmed down, creative, and energized in the times of solitude and silence that I build into my daily routines. I'm exhausted after exchanges with groups who are there to mingle and chitchat. I don't "entertain" people at dinner parties. I'm not a great cook. And even if I were, I really don't like to cook.

So, what is someone like me doing in the practice of spiritual direction where hospitality is front and center? I'm here because spiritual direction has helped me redefine what true hospitality looks and feels like. Up until I entered spiritual direction and began training to become a director, I never would have claimed I had the gift of hospitality. Now I believe it is one of my strongest gifts, or at least it is the one I'm most passionate about and is a growth edge for me. A listening heart and an attentive mind are the greatest gifts of hospitality anyone can offer another person. Hospitality reflects the welcoming heart of God and lives out Jesus' invitation, "Come to me and I will give you rest" (Matt. 11:28, AP). This gift is the key that opens all the other gifts because we simply can't respond to the invitation to a deeper journey until we feel welcomed, safe, and at ease.

GETTING COMFORTABLE WITH A SPIRITUAL DIRECTOR

If you're new to the idea of spiritual direction, the very term itself can feel inhospitable and cause you to raise an eyebrow of suspicion. It may sound like surrendering control of your spiritual life to a spiritual boss who hands out assignments and homework to make you a better pray-er, more patient, or anything else they think you need to be "more spiritual." If any of this were the reality, I would recommend running away as far and as fast as you can, and I would be right behind you. In truth, a spiritual director is more of an observer, a companion on the journey who will walk with you, listen to you, be silent with you, laugh or cry with you, and be the lookout in you for Christ, the "author and perfecter of your faith" (Heb. 12:2, AP).

Metaphors help to describe the role of spiritual director and the practice of direction. For instance, Margaret Guenther expounds on the metaphor of the director as a midwife who helps another give birth to what is growing or awakening within her.[1] I like that image because it acknowledges that the life within the directee does not belong to the midwife, and the midwife is not the one laboring to bring forth new life. Yet she is a present help, a comforter, encourager, and observer of the process who is aware of changes, challenges, and the stages of birth.

However, I've recently begun to prefer to think of a spiritual director as a musical director who neither writes the music nor performs it. The director listens, observes, tunes the ear, blends the notes into a harmonious whole, and highlights spots of dissonance or hurried rhythms. The director may tone down the brassy voices that have led the melody for too long so that the quieter voices can find their full beauty and expression. The role of the director is to offer a greater perspective and attunement to how one is participating in the divine symphony.

Only when I have this image of spiritual direction firmly set in my mind can I feel at home in that holy, blessed, welcoming, and safe place with a person who joyfully, lovingly, and without judgment receives me and my story. Once we understand this relationship, we can become hospitable to our own journey by choosing to trust the companion and the process as we settle into conversation. That is simply all that spiritual direction is—a sacred conversation between two people, focused on the dialogue between the Divine and the directee.

A WELCOMING SPACE

Setting a welcoming tone is critical to the relationship between the director and directee. Every director I've met with over the years has their own way of creating those first welcoming moments. A quiet space free from distractions and an element of privacy typically work best. However, I've met with directees, usually younger people, who feel safer and more relaxed in public spaces like a coffee shop, park, library, or even out walking together on the street.

I first saw that it is possible to welcome someone in public places long before my spiritual direction experiences began. Back when my introverted daughter was a teenager, we were navigating the challenges in our home following my divorce. Most days she was sullen, somber, or downright angry at life, if not at me in particular. Yet once a week we seemed to have an "unplanned" connection, but not a typical sit-down-to-talk kind of meeting. It happened nearly every Saturday when she would come with me to do the grocery shopping.

Something about her pushing the cart and my gathering the food allowed her to talk, really talk, about what was going on with her and her friends, school, and other family concerns. I mostly listened, asked an occasional question, and listened again. Our movements through the grocery aisles became our liturgy of deeper connection that I treasure to this day, and she fondly remembers.

This is an example of the diverse and creative ways that people find their safe places. But ideally a direction relationship offers a quiet, set-apart, sanctified time and space. The key is to honor and respect the desire of the one seeking companionship in exploring the landscape of their soul. A routine of welcoming, greeting, and checking in with each other begins most sessions. The director may offer a cup of tea, coffee, or water, and then the session begins with a settling-in routine.

I like to start sessions with what I call a "gathering silence"—a time for the director and directee to take a breath, close their eyes for a minute, gather thoughts, and release stress. When the directee is ready to begin the conversation, they end the silence with a simple "amen." I have found this to be a comfortable welcome for most people, but every director finds their own way of welcoming a directee. I personally have loved the variety of hospitable gestures and have felt that each of my directors took time to consider my unique personality and story.

Some directors simply light a candle as symbol of the Spirit's presence. Some read an opening prayer, blessing, psalm, or poem. A brief guided Centering Prayer, a meditation, or some quiet music can settle the soul. Whatever the practice, physical comfort and hospitality to body and soul set the stage for the conversation. Don't hesitate to let your director know if a particular style of welcome is uncomfortable in any way. This is *your* hour to process your life and your faith journey, and your director will want to know how to best help you.

In some situations, a director may meet with directees over the phone or a video chat platform. Being in different locations may necessitate some alteration to the welcoming routine, but it is still important to create a sense of welcome.

WELCOMING CONVERSATION

When first finding a spiritual director, it is important to meet with two or three directors to determine where you feel most comfortable (see the information in appendix 5). After I moved to a new region of the country, I set out to find my new spiritual director. A friend referred me to a woman, but she was slow to respond to email. I don't expect immediate responses to my emails, but I sent a second message after a week of silence. Several more days passed before she wrote and explained she had out-of-town visitors and apologized for the slow response. We agreed on a meeting, and indeed it seemed she would be a delightful companion. However, my sense that she was unavailable or unresponsive was the first clue that this was not the welcoming relationship I needed at that time.

On our next visit, I began to talk through the challenges of my move and transitioning into a comfortable rhythm of life. The change in culture—everything from clothing to politics, weather, and landscape—was extreme in every way. When I talked about feeling like a stranger trying to get my bearings, she began to share her views of the local environment and questioned why I would ever feel like a stranger in such an open-minded culture. I immediately felt on the defensive as she continued to share her opinions. Although I had not specifically shared what my views were, her bold declaration of where she stood on the political scene was enough to shut down that conversation and for me to quickly change the topic.

I don't believe for a minute that she wanted to make me feel unwelcome. That was my own doing, my state of mind and response at the time. I do expect my director to challenge my thinking at times. But in this first conversation, I easily discerned that I needed a spiritual companion who could allow me to explore and discover at my own pace and in my own way, someone with the grace to hold my views even if they are contrary to their own. This was the only time I've ever felt I couldn't meet with a director.

A spiritual director should also be working to discern whether the relationship will be an open and welcoming one for the directee. I once had an initial meeting with a woman who had a background in New Age spirituality and was seeking a director on her spiritual path. I would have been happy to journey with her, but we just weren't speaking the same language. Even during our one conversation, I had to ask her to explain what she meant by many of the phrases she used. And she told me how uncomfortable she was to hear the divine cosmos referred to with a male pronoun.

I knew I would be on edge and self-conscious in a continuing relationship, trying to avoid her trigger words that I had grown up with, while embracing a new spiritual language that sounded odd to my ears. It felt awkward, and we mutually agreed it was not the best fit, although we both thoroughly enjoyed the conversation and the company. I sent her off with blessings for the journey and trust she found her place to be at home in spiritual direction.

This first stage of developing a welcoming conversation and feeling at ease may take some time as you become comfortable sharing your personal journey with another person. It also takes time to welcome the gift of someone being present with you on your journey, especially if you've felt alone in your spiritual development. Once you find that person, the conversation begins to unfold naturally. In getting to know you as a directee, some directors will ask about your specific areas of spiritual formation to better understand your personal journey. They may ask how you experience prayer. They will likely ask about your understanding of who God is and how that has changed over time. They may ask about your current or past church experiences and how they have affected you.

Other directors will simply ask you to share what led you to seek a director and what you hope to experience in such a relationship. Every person brings a different hope or desire to their first encounter with direction. Some examples include exploration of something yet unknown, a more authentic relationship with God, a place to talk about some doubts in their faith, better relationships, a more integrated life, new ways to pray, and discernment of calling. These and a thousand other reasons send us out to find a safe place to draw close to God.

PRACTICING HOSPITALITY

In a society that considers self-care selfish or a waste of time, we must fight the inner voice that says we don't deserve to spend time talking about ourselves to a spiritual companion or reflecting on life and how God is meeting us. We say things like, "There are so many other things I could be doing for others. . . . So many other things I need to be accomplishing." But we would never say these things to a friend who asked to talk about something that was going on with them. We are quick to encourage, comfort, and welcome other people. Why are we so inhospitable to our own souls?

Resistance Inventory. Look at the resistance you encounter as you welcome yourself into the dialogue of your inner being. How have you deflected the care and attention your heart is seeking? Write down the negative, inhospitable messages that surface in your mind. Trace the origin of such messages in your life. What do these voices sound like? Now, rather than trying to make them go away, simply invite them to take a back seat and sit quietly while you develop a new message, new posture, new attitude toward welcoming yourself into the loving presence of God. Write a new message of welcome over the top of the old inhospitable messages you just wrote. Then rewrite the new message again on a fresh page in your journal. Seal that message by contemplating the importance of your inner being that Paul described in Ephesians 3:16-17:

> I pray that, according to the riches of his glory, he may grant that you may be strengthened in your inner being with power through his Spirit, and that Christ may dwell in your hearts through faith, as you are being rooted and grounded in love.

As you make your way toward grace-filled hospitality, you may eventually notice those inhospitable voices have left the room. Then you can relax as you journey together with your spiritual director, knowing that where two or three are gathered in Jesus' name, there he is, ready to welcome you joyfully as you launch into the divine unknown.

SACRED CONVERSATION

- How do you define *hospitality*? Think about an experience where you felt fully welcomed and at home. Write about that experience in your journal using all five senses—sight, hearing, touch, smell, and taste.
- Consider the times and circumstances where you have felt unwelcome. How has this sense of being unwelcome affected you (your desire to welcome others in a better way than you have experienced, your ability to trust others, your openness to intimacy, etc.)? What insights do you learn about yourself as you reflect on these two sides of hospitality—welcome and unwelcome?
- How hospitable have you felt to your own journey through life? Do you welcome your story, or are you hard on yourself? Consider Jesus' invitation to welcome your own soul on this faith journey. How would you respond to this invitation?

> Are you tired? Worn out? Burned out on religion? Come to me. Get away with me and you'll recover your life. I'll show you how to take a real rest. Walk with me and work with me—watch how I do it. Learn the unforced rhythms of grace. I won't lay anything heavy or ill-fitting on you. Keep company with me and you'll learn to live freely and lightly. (Matt. 11:28-29, THE MESSAGE)

- What do you most need from God so you can experience the gift of hospitality?

three

The Gift of Story

Your life, my life, is given graciously by God. Our lives are not problems to be solved but journeys to be taken with Jesus as our friend and finest guide.

—Henri J. M. Nouwen, *Spiritual Direction*

We've all experienced this scenario: You're in a meeting at work, or listening to a sermon at church, or attending a workshop or classroom lecture. The speaker is sharing information, concepts, theories, doctrines, and you are barely listening. Then the speaker shares a personal story from the heart. It could be a heartbreaking story, a funny situation, an extraordinary happening, or an ordinary occurrence.

The moment they turn to the personal, a holy hush settles over the room. People look up from their papers, books, or cell phones. They make eye contact with the speaker. They stop what they are doing and listen, drawn in by the story, and they now know the speaker in a new way. Why? Because a life is a gift, a story captivating; someone risking vulnerability, breathtaking. When these moments happen, we are changed, the storyteller is changed, and our hearts are opened, connected, and alive to possibility.

The holiness of storytelling is revealed by the words of the apostle Paul: "Present your bodies as a living sacrifice, holy and acceptable to God, which is your spiritual worship" (Rom. 12:1). Our bodies are the vessels in which we live out the stories of our lives, and our physical embodiment reflects God's image in the world. Only when we embrace all we have experienced as human beings—from our heartbreaking agonies to our ecstatic victories—and freely return them to God can they be used for our healing and as a part of the story on our journey.

THE CHALLENGE

Accepting the idea of story as holy ground is one thing, but applying it to our own lives is entirely another. It may feel too self-centered. Yet human life—incarnate, in-the-flesh living—is not self-centered but God-centered. The point of meditating on your own life story isn't to judge it as dull, ordinary, or not worth sharing. Nor is it to turn it into a bestselling memoir to impress friends and family. Embracing and exploring your own life certainly isn't self-serving or narcissistic. The point is to receive every minute of your life as gift and then offer it all back to God whose tender mercies cover your heart, mind, and soul.

In *Spiritual Exercises*, the founder of the Jesuits, Saint Ignatius of Loyola, offers this prayer that speaks of all of life as an offering to God:

> Take Lord, and receive all my liberty, my memory, my understanding, and all my will—all that I have and possess. You, Lord, have given all that to me. I now give it back to you, O Lord. All of it is yours. Dispose of it according to your will. Give me love of yourself along with your grace, for that is enough for me.[1]

Once you accept the power of your life story and recognize it as holy gift, how exactly do you sink down into it and discern what it all means and how it has brought you to this point? Where do you begin to recognize and share you own story?

I find it best to consider story as part of the ongoing, eternal flow of the Spirit of God in our world. Understanding that grace and truth have followed me all the days of my life allows me to consider the essential element of spiritual storytelling: God has been at work from my past to this present moment with grace always paving the way for my next steps into the future.

THE PAST

Before you begin recalling or recording the story of your life, start with a few minutes of silence and stillness before God. Ask the Spirit to guide you in all wisdom, teaching you all that you need to know, remember, and offer. Ask for divine protection to surround you as you recall and capture your memories. I also encourage you to share your intention with a friend, pastor, or your spiritual director if you already have one. Ask that person to pray for you during this process.

Looking back over the years allows you to identify how life has been leading, speaking, and teaching you. As Parker Palmer writes, "Before you tell your life what you intend to do with it, listen for what it intends to do with you."[2] Entering into memories can feel painful, yet the inner work of healing and wholeness requires that we take time to remember.

This regathering of life, especially sharing it with another, can give rise to fear, sorrow, regret, and mourning over wounds or losses. One woman I know began gathering her story to share with a small listening group and quickly encountered intense emotions that left her weepy for most of the week as she brought out sorrowful events that she had long buried. I always assure people in this process that they do not have to tell their story to someone else. The person who most needs to hear and embrace your story as sacred is you.

By the end of a week of tearful processing, my friend felt ready to share the story and was forever changed, not only by the telling but also by the embrace of love and grace from the group where she shared it. Indeed, what had felt like hurt and wounding led her to reconciliation and a sense of wholeness she had not expected or experienced before. It gave her a confidence in her own story and in God's faithfulness through it all.

I learned to love remembering my past—including the sometimes-painful memories—by meditating on the word *remember* itself. *Re-member.* If all our faculties—the literal "members" of our body, including our memories, senses, emotions, personality, and physical being—remain disconnected from our consciousness, we become out of joint, separated from the whole, "dis-membered" or "dis-integrated." The re-membering is a way of re-integrating all the parts and pieces into the dwelling place of God and experiencing divine healing. Only then do we begin to experience the abundant life Jesus promised.

Give yourself permission to express your story as you feel comfortable and to take as much time as you need. Sometimes one memory or season of life can take days or weeks to unpack. A journal is a good place to start. If you are unaccustomed to or uncomfortable with writing it all out, at least create an outline of highs and lows as a starting point. Then consider using one of the following ideas to prompt your recollection.

Photo Gallery. Gather photographs from throughout your life. Lay them out on a table and let them speak to you. Which images make you wonder about something? Which evoke an emotion in you? Which capture significant events in your life? Now look at them as a whole collection. What kind of childhood experience do these images express? What do you notice consistently in many of the photos? Is mom always serious? Is dad always laughing? How do you look in each image? Are you engaged, shy, free-spirited, or prim and proper? Jot down thoughts and insights you gain from this visual display.

Time Line. On a large piece of paper, draw a time line horizontally through the middle of the page. Mark the beginning of the line with the year you were born and the end with the current year. Above the line, pinpoint specific events in cultural or world history. These can be political events, disasters, inventions, deaths of famous people, etc. Below the line, note the highlights of your own life in five- or ten-year increments. As you review these events and see your life in the context of the history of the world, what do you notice? How do you feel? Are there any connections between the historic events and your life events? What highlights were more life changing than others? Once you've meditated on this representation of your life, write some of your thoughts and truths in your journal.

Networks. Some people experience life in a more social or relational context than others. As you move through your life story, note the people who have had the most impact, positive or negative, on the formation of your life and your attitudes throughout the years. What are the common threads that have created a lifeline for you?

Maps. Another perspective is based on the places you've lived from birth to now. How have these locations created milestones in your growth? How have they contributed to your identity? Are there particular events that led you to a new chapter of life or a new understanding?

THE PRESENT-DAY STORY

Having re-membered your life story, you come to the present reality. Here you encounter the ongoing work of living an intentional, examined life. As you spend more time with a spiritual director, these are often the kind of stories you bring to the session—things you are currently noticing, practicing, or discovering. The psalmist wrote one of the earliest prayers of Examen, "Search me, O God, and know my heart; test me and know my thoughts. See if there is any wicked way in me, and lead me in the way everlasting" (Ps. 139:23-24). There are numerous ways to embrace your life story as it is unfolding each day, partnering with God as you consider, *How is it with my soul?*

The Examen. Ignatius adapted this form of daily prayer in the *Spiritual Exercises* by expanding it to include an Examen of Conscience and an Examen of Consciousness. The Examen of Conscience recalls those things that weigh on us, asking God for awareness and mercy for the things we have done and the things we have left undone. The Examen of Consciousness is slightly different, asking that we become aware of all that has passed through our day: the spiritual, physical, emotional, and social aspects of life. The Daily Examen typically takes only a few minutes using the following simple flow:

- *Remember:* Ask God to bring to your mind the highlights and details of your day—allowing the day to pass through your thoughts rather than trying to recount every hour or minute. Thank God for each remembrance and receive it as gift.
- *Reflect:* Be aware of any significant feelings—positive or negative—that arise in this review of the day and consider what has drawn you closer to God, spurring growth or consolation through faith, hope, and love. These may be times when you feel most alive, engaged, inspired, or enthused. Then consider any decision, attitude, judgment, or frustration that may have led you away from God. Recognize these times by the doubts, confusion, and anxiety they have produced.
- *Receive:* Holding these remembrances before God, give thanks and rejoice in it all. Seek forgiveness where

needed. Receive and rejoice in God's outpouring of grace and mercy throughout your day.

- *Restore:* Finally, offer these insights as steppingstones to tomorrow and all that will pass your way. Ask for the grace or gift you will need to meet tomorrow. As you are led, record any insights, commitments, hopes, or joys in your journal.

Landscapes. One of my favorite ways to explore my life story is by considering the landscape of my soul. This is always a much easier exercise if I am regularly engaged in the prayer of Daily Examen. I review my journal for the week or month as I prepare for a spiritual direction session. From this review I consider the landscape. I may be wandering in a desert or isolated in a dense forest, unconnected from others. I may be walking through a garden, or I may experience a season of fruitfulness and imagine an orchard of fruit trees. I sometimes find an image online that represents my chosen landscape, and I sit with that image, offering the scene to God, asking God to lead me through it or bring to my mind God's view of this landscape of my soul. Bringing concrete images or metaphors into your life story can help you express and deepen the reality of God at work in it all.

Five-Moment Memoir. This is another approach to the prayer of Examen. Think through your day and consider five moments. They can be anything—a conversation, a kindness, a hurt, a reading—from the tiniest observance of a bug on a window to a major news event. You decide; then jot down those five moments in your journal without much detail.

Now sit with those specific moments and hold them in silent prayer. What do you notice? Is there a commonality to them?

Determine which one resonates with you the most, stirring up a positive or negative emotion. Begin journaling about this moment using all five senses to describe the details of how it occurred or what you observed. What are your emotional, physical, and spiritual responses to that moment? What questions does it prompt? What wisdom does it reveal?

After you've written all you have to say, spend a few minutes in silence, offering this moment to God and listening for promptings. What do you take into your future from this prayer encounter? End your prayer with thanksgiving or a simple word of gratitude in your journal.

PROVIDENTIAL GRACE

Finally, the story of our lives has a future that we cannot fully see, but we can be assured that God has already been there preparing the place and the path for us. This is providential grace. We can recognize this reality as we look back and recognize the fingerprints of God on it all. And while we can't know the future in full, I believe our hearts' desires, planted within us by the Spirit, prepare us to live our best life.

What does your heart desire in your life today? Is it a sense of calling? Maybe you want relief from a difficult challenge or confusion. Where does the desire lead? Is it toward God's wisdom, grace, and love, or does it take you away from God into areas of hurt, revenge, or addictive habits? All desires, positive or negative, turned toward God become acts of prayer and opportunities to listen to the Divine calling us to follow in some way.

Not long ago, I wanted to be more deeply engaged in my spiritual direction practice. I considered how to do that, sat with the question and the desire for months, and considered many options, all of them good and exciting opportunities to live more deeply into my calling. But occasionally this desire felt like it conflicted with another desire and calling to return to my writing. For a long time, I considered these desires as mutually exclusive. Which one would I follow? These were the questions of discernment that I often brought up in my meeting with my spiritual director. Ultimately and quite suddenly, these two desires merged into one as they found a place to dwell together in the words that you now read. God's kindness led me to this connection and new combination of desires by preparing my heart, mind, and talents to do exactly what I wanted to do all along.

Story is holy ground. Life is divine gift. Honoring the past, present, and future is our greatest calling and opportunity to live the God-imagined abundant life.

SACRED CONVERSATION

- Underline words or phrases in this chapter that stir a response within you. Do you feel resistant to an idea? Are you encouraged, excited, curious, or feeling some other way?
- What has been your attitude in the past to the idea of telling your life story? How has that attitude changed after reading through this chapter?
- What obstacles (internal or external) arise as you consider sharing your story?

- In considering how you might express your life story, or how you have done so in the past, what methods of expression are you most drawn to? How might you begin this exercise of re-membering your story?
- What do you need from God to help you open the gift of story?

four

The Gift of Pilgrimage

What will ground us is a commitment to return to the center even as we travel life's edges. . . . There is no map. We can only drop deep into our hearts to guide us through our next steps.

—Christine Valters Paintner, *The Soul of a Pilgrim*

Spiritual direction creates a place to rest as we make pilgrimage through the new territory of the inner life. Resting and refueling are always parts of a pilgrimage, but sometimes we overlook them. The spiritual journey is not just about walking and checking off miles. Pilgrimage also calls us to savor the journey and reflect as we wander.

Spiritual direction asks us to pause, to not be so concerned about getting somewhere specific or about the speed we are progressing. When I first began to meet with a director, I experienced our monthly meeting not only as a time to reflect on my spiritual life and relationship with God but also as a physical respite from the survival-mode mentality I had adopted as I acclimated to life as a single parent.

This hour allowed me to look back where I had been, reflect, and ask myself and God questions about what I had seen and experienced. *What do I need to grieve? What could I release and celebrate?* These and many other questions arise as we explore life and faith and God. Such questions are found throughout the scriptures because these sacred stories are all about journey and resting as we come to know ourselves and God.

Beginning in the Creation story, God walked in the Garden with Adam and Eve. But after they chose to veer off the path offered by their Creator, God continued walking in the Garden "at the time of the evening breeze," calling to them, "Where are you?" (Gen. 3:8-9).

Hagar ran away into the desert to escape the heartache and cruelty she experienced as Abraham and Sarah's servant. But an angel met her there and asked, "Where are you going?" (Gen. 16:8).

Elijah, having fled for forty days and forty nights into the wilderness in fear of Queen Jezebel, eventually ended up hiding in a cave. The Lord came to him and asked, "What are you doing here, Elijah?" (1 Kings 19:9).

Jesus came upon two disciples on their way to Emmaus and he asked, "What are you discussing with each other while you walk along?" (Luke 24:17).

It takes time to sit with the weight of such questions, listening to what stirs. *Where are you? Where are you going? What are you doing here? What are you discussing as you walk along?* These questions lie at the heart of conversations with a spiritual director. And from the responses of these spiritual ancestors, we gain clues about how we may experience the journey. Adam and Eve hid from God and made guilt-ridden excuses. Hagar ran away from trouble but listened to God's prompting to return to make peace. Elijah simply wanted to give up and hid his face in his cloak. The two disciples stumbled along in the darkness of their disappointment until Jesus opened their eyes and they recognized him within their own "burning hearts."

These examples acknowledge the multiple pathways and unique responses. Spiritual direction allows us to discern the questions we need to sit with on our journey and consider how we will respond to the path set before us.

WONDERING AND WANDERING

One of the most meaningful gifts I've experienced in sharing the journey with a spiritual director is the invitation to wonder as I wander. This wondering helps me see what I am experiencing in a new light, often a light that arises within myself as I stop to consider new perspectives. Let me give you an example.

One of the things that first drove me to spiritual direction was my awareness that I had lost my connection to any emotion about life. As I shared this "blankness" in my life over the course of two or three sessions, my director said something like, "I wonder if there might be another truth about your lack of emotion that you might consider."

I sat in silence for a minute and then shrugged my shoulders. "I don't know," I eventually responded.

"Would it be okay if we just sat together silently for a while, listening for any kind of movement about this?" she asked.

I nodded yes and closed my eyes, asking God for anything that would help me see this more clearly. Within a few seconds a thought was given. I say "given" because it was something I had never thought of before. I was so surprised by it that I gave a little cry of "Oh!" Then I said, "It seems that while I've been trying to survive, God has simply been holding my emotions safe like a treasure to protect me from falling to pieces while I rearrange my life for me and my daughters."

My director smiled and nodded. "Does that make a difference in how you see what's happening in your life?"

"It changes everything," I said. "I literally feel physically lighter, hopeful, protected, and loved by God."

And it did change everything. Soon thereafter I slowly began to regain my emotional balance and connection to people and situations and life. This is the gentle way of direction that encourages us to look, wonder, and look again at a situation or emotion or attitude, to not pave over the rough spots or take long detours to avoid a thorny patch.

When invited by a director to wonder about something, it's also okay to say, "No, I want to move to another topic." This is your journey. But once the wondering begins, it typically plants a seed of possibility that continues to grow over weeks and months. We often say that spiritual direction is not about what happens in that hour together but in all the hours in between that lead to transformation.

Wondering helps us step into the silence of a loving God that may open a new awareness that changes everything. However, this new thought or awareness isn't always dramatic. Often "wondering" is a tool I take with me as I leave my session, making me more thoughtful about a situation or an attitude that eventually leads to a slow transformation. I like to keep the words of Pierre Teilhard de Chardin close at hand, especially when I'm feeling impatient about this slow pilgrimage:

> Above all, trust in the *slow* work of God. We are, quite naturally, impatient in everything to reach the end without delay. We should like to skip the intermediate stages. We are impatient of being *on the way to* something *unknown,* something *new.* And yet it is the law of all progress that it is made by passing through some stages of instability—and that may take a very long time. . . . Give our Lord the benefit of believing that his hand is leading you surely enough through the obscurity and the "becoming," and accept, for love of him, the anxiety of feeling yourself in suspense and incomplete.[1]

I recall sitting with a directee once who was acclimating to new terrain on her journey, shifting from work life to a retired life. All the helping skills she had used throughout her career seemed to be annoying people in her retirement. She gave several examples of how she had helped others, provided answers, and offered solutions. She used to be rewarded for her work and felt a sense of purpose. Now she felt lost as these helping habits seemed to be rejected by others.

Together we wondered if there might be another definition of "helping" in her retirement that God was inviting her to explore. In her long wondering and wandering, she began to recognize that the ways she offered hospitality and welcome to a great variety of people in her home felt like a possible new definition of "helping." This was the slow work of God, and it took courage for her to accept the anxiety of feeling herself in suspense and incomplete during the months of wondering.

SIGNPOSTS ALONG THE WAY

Another facet of this gift of pilgrimage is the underlying story behind what we present in a direction session. These signposts may be hidden to us until we uncover them in the conversation with a skilled director who can listen beyond the words we say.

For instance, I recently talked to my director about the anger and hurt I felt at my workplace due to a poorly communicated change in my role and responsibilities. I used the word *betrayal.* But as I expressed my anger, my director asked if perhaps there was an element of fear or loss to consider in this scenario. Indeed, this question became a Lookout Point signpost that helped me see beyond the face of anger to a new perspective on my fear of losing my job, coupled with my perceived loss of status. The view of that fear led to a completely different conversation and awareness of God working with me and in me to calm the storm.

In other circumstances, my director has pointed out Detour signs, where I've sidetracked my own journey by shrugging off sorrow as no big deal or minimizing my own pain by comparing it to that of others who have it much worse. Noticing these signposts with a skilled director invites me to return to my own journey, my own sorrows and pain points.

Occasionally I will present facts and information about what I'm learning in life based on knowledge alone. This Information Ahead signpost asks that I stop and consider how new knowledge is changing the way I think, behave, or feel about something. In other words, how do I get the knowledge that is in my head to inhabit my heart and my body?

LIFE ON PILGRIMAGE

So how might we experience the gift of pilgrimage as more than a metaphor? How can this expression of the spiritual journey be a tool for sharing in our spiritual direction sessions? Traditionally, pilgrimage includes traveling to historic holy spots such as the Holy Land or hiking the Camino de Santiago in Spain or other paths to places of sacred remembrance. Less traditional pilgrimages are through national parks or along marked trails as a means of letting go of baggage and learning to travel light on life's journey.

These pilgrimage-type journeys can be deeply meaningful and formative but are not typically a part of the daily and weekly spiritual life and journey. Our challenge then is to keep our hearts engaged in the pilgrim journey through our ordinary days. Or as is beautifully expressed in the Psalms, "Blessed are those whose strength is in you, whose hearts are set on pilgrimage" (Ps. 84:5, NIV). I suggest the following tools for a regular engagement with being on pilgrimage.

Journaling. Let's begin here because the root word for *journal* and *journey* is the same, meaning "a place of progress." I understand that not everyone loves writing in a journal as much as I do.

I understand it's difficult, awkward, and may bring up memories of your fifth-grade teacher making nasty comments about your writing. But let's agree that this baggage is something we can now release as we enter a new adventure where writing is free-flowing and becomes prayer. Only you and God will read your journal, and God absolutely adores you and your expressions in your journal, even if it's written in crayon, as bullet-point to-do lists, or with fits and starts of words and phrases with bad grammar and angry rants. This is all of you on the page, and that's a beautiful thing.

Writing is a miraculous thing really. There is something of divine mystery that shows up at the tip of a pen moving across the page, connecting thoughts (mind) to movement down the arm and to the hand (body) to reveal hidden and often surprising truths that give rise to a holy "yes" or "aha" (heart). Not every word we write gives us that jolt of new truth. Sometimes it takes a page or two of free writing or stream-of-consciousness writing to enter the creative flow. But even those pages of scattered thoughts become for me a gathering prayer (like the gathering silence mentioned in the Gift of Hospitality). This free writing brings together the shards of a fractured existence into one sacred space on the page. For me, the pilgrimage through my days needs this kind of attention to unwrap all that God wants to reveal to me.

Also consider the pace of writing. Generally, most people talk at around 200 to 250 words per minute. Most can type somewhere between 80 and 120 words per minute. But writing slows us down to a mere 30 to 40 words per minute. When I've given retreats focused on journaling, many people tell me they prefer to write on their computers because they can't get the words down on paper fast enough to keep up with their thoughts. For me, that's the entire point of handwriting. Yes, a thought or two may slip away before I can capture it, but if it's vital, it will return. If it isn't, I let it go.

I like to imagine the slow rhythm of writing that engages body, mind, and spirit as if it were a handheld folded fan. Most of the time, the fan is folded up tight because of the speed at which we live. But when we write, the fan begins to unfold, and the thoughts, ideas, and emotions caught deep within the folds are now exposed and find room to breathe and be heard. This is why we come to new thoughts and ideas that startle us awake with an affirmative "Amen, so be it." This is our place of progress and transformation.

The Labyrinth. Many retreat centers, churches, and even some parks have prayer labyrinths. Walking the labyrinth has been a part of the Christian tradition of prayer and meditation for centuries. It typically takes a circular path with one entrance point at the outer edge and winds back and forth, spiraling around the circle until it reaches the entrance into an inner space or circle. The only way out (other than just cutting through all the paths) is to walk the same path you entered.

This gentle rhythm of slowly moving from external to internal and back out again symbolizes the spiritual path moving ever nearer to the inner being, the abiding place of God. There is no one way to use the labyrinth. Each time I walk one, the experience takes on a life of its own. Sometimes I bring something with me for the journey, an offering or a prayer symbol to leave at the center space, often adding it to dozens of other offerings from others who have walked this path.

Or I may walk a prayer of praise. I recall one such pilgrimage around the labyrinth when the stone markers along the path seemed to represent the great cloud of witnesses who join me on my journey. They seemed to be applauding me as I walked, encouraging me. I remembered as many of them as I could and offered prayers of gratitude for their companionship and teaching throughout my life. The prayer path could also represent a season of transformation over a certain period, acknowledging the slow change from the outside in and inside out.

Neighborhood Pilgrimage. As I write these words, we are in the midst of shelter-in-place orders to curb the spread of the COVID-19 pandemic. While we can't gather with groups of people during this season, we can get out to walk our neighborhoods. This is the perfect daily or weekly pilgrimage to pray through your neighborhood for those you know and those who are strangers, for a spirit of unity, strength, health, and kindness to permeate our streets and strengthen our families. You may also want simply to walk in awareness of anything that catches your attention or resonates with you. Capture a picture of it with your cell phone to reflect on throughout the week or month.

Pilgrimage calls us to wander, wonder, and welcome the journey inward and the journey outward. It calls us to take another step closer to the heart of God that is beating inside us. It asks that we stretch, climb, walk, run, and rest in the green pastures or the valley of shadows, knowing that others have walked the path before us, others will follow us, and still others walk with us today as spiritual companions on the pilgrim way.

SACRED CONVERSATION

- Underline those words or phrases in this chapter that stir an emotion in you.
- Read Psalm 23. Using it as a guide, where are you on your faith pilgrimage? Notice the variety of different pathways this writer travels—green pastures, quiet streams, valley of the shadow of death, the house of the Lord—but in the end is the realization that "surely goodness and mercy shall follow me all the days of my life" (v. 6). As you reflect on your journey, where do you recognize God's goodness and mercy traveling with you?
- As you consider creative expressions of your faith pilgrimage, what are you drawn to? Does an artistic endeavor appeal to you? Starting a new journal? Finding or creating a labyrinth? What are the possibilities for pilgrimage in your region? In your faith community?
- Who are the spiritual companions who have been traveling with you? Family, friends, mentors, pastors, writers? How might a spiritual direction relationship bring a new dimension to your journey?

five

The Gift of Silence

Silence is an urgent necessity for us; silence is necessary if we are to hear God speaking in eternal silence. Our own silence is necessary if God is to hear us.

—MARTIN LAIRD, *INTO THE SILENT LAND*

I used to have a problem with silence. Since I had worked long and hard at finding my voice, silence felt like regressing. But being *silent* is different from being *silenced.* I have come to realize that silence has its own voice. It is a voice of strength and confidence, contentment and peace, trust and surrender. It is the voice of truth and grace that embraces my gifts as well as my weaknesses. Silence is more than an absence of noise. It's an inner quality of being centered in oneself, connected to the Divine Presence at work within the soul.

Silence is space to breathe, to enter an expansive grace. Silence fasts from the need to say something about everything or something about nothing. Silence graciously opens space for others to speak and to find their own voice without imposing perspectives or opinions on them.

THE SILENT PRESENCE

Silence is the lifeblood of spiritual direction. You may wonder how that can be if the idea is to engage in conversation about all manner of life, love, loss, and longing. But silence is the gift offered by the director who sits and listens unhurried and silently present to your unfolding story. After sharing what is on my mind and in my heart during that hour with my director, I often come to a point where I feel done or emptied, and I fall silent. At first, this may feel awkward because our culture teaches us to keep conversations going. However, in spiritual direction, the conversation ebbs and flows. I find these spaces of silence become a bridge from my head to my heart as I listen inwardly to what I have just shared.

I love when a director doesn't rush to respond but gives space for my thoughts to see if anything else remains for me to say. Sometimes a director will acknowledge the in-between silence and say, "Let's hold what you've shared for a minute in silence." Or they may gently circle back to a word or a phrase that seemed to hold some weight. A director's listening skills can hear it, hold it, and re-present it with a simple, "Can you say more about that?" And I begin again and go further into the heart of the matter.

Setting aside an hour each month to breathe, meditate on life, reflect, and simply sit in silence is a life-giving, soul-restoring practice in this incessantly noisy world.

SILENT SURRENDER

The prophet Isaiah wrote, "In quietness and in trust shall be your strength" (Isa. 30:15). The essence of practicing silence and stillness centers on trusting God. Those words, *trusting God*, have become the trite answer to anyone's current dilemma. "Just trust God." But when coupled with quietness or silence the phrase becomes something altogether different. This is about an intimate relationship with God. What does it mean to trust God in quietness? It means—even when I feel confused or alone or stirred up—I stake my claim in God's promise to never leave me and always work for my good. It means I trust God's grace when I think I'm missing the mark or feel that I'm falling behind.

In silence we surrender ourselves, but this is not possible unless we are in a safe place. Surrender is vulnerable, unguarded, stripped down. According to the writer of Hebrews, "Before [God] no creature is hidden, but all are naked and laid bare" (4:13). Putting ourselves in this vulnerable state is a choice, and silence is the way we say yes to God by trusting God with our lives.

While quiet, simple trust and surrender can sometimes be frightening, they can also be a relief. A few years ago when I was struggling with a decision about my career, I woke up one morning with this prayer on my lips: "You are the God of my undoing." It surprised me that this had come to me as the first thought on my waking, but even more surprising was my comfort with this new name for God. It was almost a rejoicing or a relief, as if I were inviting God to undo what I had tied up in knots in my life, undo the knots that kept me bound up in my own head and habits. I welcomed the relief of surrendering anything God wanted to undo in me. This prayer has stayed with me ever since.

Martin Laird describes this beautifully in a way that sounds like Isaiah's promise that "in quietness and in trust shall be your strength" (30:15):

> Contemplative practice [silence and stillness] doesn't acquire anything. . . . [I]t is not a technique but a surrendering of deeply imbedded resistances that allows the sacred within gradually to reveal itself as a simple, fundamental fact. Out of this letting go there emerges what St. Paul called our "hidden self": "may he give you the power through his Spirit for your hidden self to grow strong."[1]

Being silent and surrendering our own agendas challenges us in so many ways because our culture operates with an I-can-do-anything mentality. We are a conquering, overcoming, building, expanding, succeeding kind of people—all commendable qualities but only as they arise out of trust in God alone.

SILENCE THAT BEARS WITNESS

Bearing witness is an old-fashioned phrase that asks us to attend to someone or something, be it a circumstance, an event, or our own inner thoughts. It's another form of what we frequently call *awareness*, or what Jesus might suggest as the call to *watch and pray*. This silent awareness partnered with prayer stands at the intersection of heaven and earth. This is the same spot where a spiritual director stands as they listen to our wanderings. And it is the seat we take in this world as participants in the ordinary sacrament of daily life.

Several years ago, I awoke to sirens and lights from the highway bridge over the lake near where I lived. I got up to look and opened a window from my second-story apartment. A mere two hundred yards away in the silence before dawn officers were yelling and running back and forth under the streetlights, looking over the bridge into the water sixty feet below. "Where is he? Where did he go?" With flashlights they saw a man in the water. Panic rose up in one officer's voice as he shouted louder, "Float on your back! Kick your feet! Don't give up!" I also heard the man in the dark water struggling. No words, just groans, gasps, the fight for life echoing beneath that bridge. The struggle continued another minute at most, but then there was silence. Dozens of police cars and fire trucks arrived on the bridge, but all of us were out of reach of this man. A few minutes later a police boat arrived with divers who pulled the lifeless body from the lake and sped away. News the next morning told me that this young man had been arrested for DUI, handcuffed, and escorted to the police car when he bolted and jumped from the bridge before the officer could catch him.

I was unable to sleep thinking of the helpless horror I had just witnessed. But as I sat with that reality before God, I began to sense it as an invitation to bear witness to this man's life . . . to his last breath . . . feeling in some way that he hadn't died alone because I and the God who dwells within me heard, saw, and honored his life and spirit in his last moments.

Bearing witness simply for the sake of watching and praying as I am able feels like a way to participate in the divine nature (see 2 Peter 1:4), to bear witness to the holy in partnership with God. Honestly, I cannot say what silently bearing witness accomplishes, and I believe those accomplishments cannot be measured in any worldly way. So I leave it in the realm of mystery. I'm not even sure what to do with this practice except to hold it and pay attention to it. The poet Mary Oliver says, "Learn to be astonished."[2] That's what happens when we enter silence with a spiritual companion who is watching and praying over our lives, honoring the moments we offer up, bearing witness to the divine nature within, and simply sitting in awe and astonishment at the wonder of God in us.

A JARRING SILENCE

During certain extremely busy or stressful times in my life, I have found it necessary, as most people do, to step away from it all and be on retreat. Whether it's a formal getaway for a personal retreat or a stay home and unplug day, retreat allows me to become aware of my comfort level with silence. Usually the busier I am, the more difficult the transition is from the fast pace into the slow, easy presence of silence. That transition can be jarring, like running over a deep pothole as I move from my daily routines into this new, silent arena. At times I've struggled to the point of wanting to pack up and return home before spending even a whole day away.

In these seasons I expect it to take several hours if not an entire day for me to feel comfortable with silence and stillness. At first, I feel edgy; sometimes I'm guilt-ridden, weepy, or I feel panic that makes me want to bolt. That's why I make sure before I go into this time alone that I have at least one support person praying for me and available to talk me down if I'm in the panicky state of mind. Some retreat centers have spiritual directors on staff who are available to meet with retreatants and can serve as a support person through the time of silence.

On an extended silent retreat in a tiny cabin in the forestland of northern Arizona, I encountered this resistance to being alone in the great silence. But I stayed with the feelings and offered them as prayer. These words I wrote in my journal still remind me that my liturgy of entering silence takes time:

> In the silence and stillness of this place, unplugged and not needed, time bends toward eternity, releasing the urgent. Pace more closely follows the speed of a cloud. I hold nothing but time as it slips from my hand into God's.
>
> It takes time to strip down to me. It takes time to put aside what was so pressing. It takes time to let the body unwind and unravel the knots of stress and demands and consuming and going. Simply stopping is in itself an offering of sacrifice to the one who brought forth time from the well of eternity and gives me a sip that tastes like hope.
>
> As evening draws the shades and light fades away, let me rest and be at peace and hear you whisper through the trees, "May all things be at rest with your soul."

THE PRACTICE OF SILENCE

How can we practice silence in everyday life, amid excessive workloads or overbooked and scattered family commitments? How do we find time and place for quietness and trust in our relationship with God? Consider these possibilities.

Centering Prayer. This is a way of praying that I "practice," but I must admit it has been difficult for me to develop as a regular daily habit. I often end the session laughing at myself for how poorly I practice it. But this is where my trust in the unseen work of the Spirit comes into play. And this is what keeps me returning to Centering Prayer.

Centering Prayer sets aside several minutes for silence and stillness, typically twenty to thirty minutes, to enter the light and love of God alone. It asks that we set aside our prayer lists, our needs, and our desires, and that we ignore the incessant thoughts that swirl in every human mind. Some use a prayer word like *peace*, *love*, or *Jesus* to keep their minds focused and turned toward God. And we let distracting thoughts float by and simply be there without engaging them in conversation. When we find our centered presence wandering away, we gently recall the prayer word to return our intention back to center, to the God who dwells within.

In this silence we attend to the love of the ever-present God. This is not the time when we seek great insights or understanding or work out theological dilemmas. This is about joining our heart, mind, and soul to the source of life and love, simply to rest and draw near the boundless love of God that is surprisingly found hidden deep in the heart of self.

I have found that this profound silence of Centering Prayer may be an exercise in frustration at first, but it has given me a vastly increased patience, the ability to let go of things—traffic, strained relationships, work demands—that would otherwise have disturbed me. I more easily let these disturbances pass through my day and give them the appropriate attention they need without being hooked into drama. For this I give God thanks and recognize God's presence in my daily life. This is also the practice that keeps me from experiencing the jarring silence I mentioned when I go on retreat. It's a practiced silence that follows me along through my days and is not a stranger when I encounter it on retreat.

The Silent Retreat. Many churches, retreat centers, or organizations offer silent retreat days to provide structure and support as you get comfortable with stillness and silence. But finding your own methods for silent retreat gives you the freedom to schedule your time and place as a regular rhythm and practice. Experiment with a liturgy for your time of quiet, weaving in prayer, scripture reading, journaling, and worship, as well as physical movement, sleep, and any other self-care you may need. Your way of retreat should feel natural, unforced, and unencumbered. (Appendix 1 offers guidelines for half-day, one-day, or extended silent retreat formats.) Here are a few of the guidelines I use for my own personal retreats.

- I come to this time willing to allow for the movement of the Spirit to change my plans.
- I bring a journal, Bible, and perhaps one book as a resource for contemplation. My book, if I bring one, doesn't focus on study or head knowledge but on something that will

open my heart to God. It may be poetry, a devotional, or something from the mystic writers.

- I unplug from technology. If it just isn't possible to leave the cell phone turned off, I limit access to it to once or twice a day for a simple check-in. No web surfing.
- I am present to the natural environment and all creation about me that God uses to display divine glory and speak to me.
- I explore a creative outlet—sketching, writing, painting, playing music, dancing, or simply gathering treasures of nature to display on a table in my room.
- I make mealtime a sacred time. Whether I eat alone or share the meal with others in a retreat center, I am present to the flavors, aromas, textures, and tastes of what God has provided to nourish my body. I eat slowly. There is no rush.
- I find a comfortable place for quiet contemplation, reading, observing, listening, waiting. I don't hold too tightly to expectations of what will happen but always welcome the Spirit to speak into my life.
- I move. Getting outside regularly to hike, walk, climb a hill, stretch, or stroll through a prayer garden or labyrinth is invigorating.
- If one is available, I meet with a spiritual director at a retreat center at the beginning of my retreat and toward the end. I talk with the director about how I am feeling going into retreat, what grace or gift I desire during this time alone with God, and how they can support me in my time of silence. At the close of retreat, I may share my

experiences, the challenges I encountered, the clarity I received, or what I take with me from this time into my everyday life.

Fasting. This is an often-overlooked form of silence that addresses specific areas of life that can become out of balance simply because we engage in them without awareness. While fasting most often refers to changing our eating habits for a brief time, it can be applied to many other habits in daily life. Ceasing to engage in these habits by fasting is a means of silencing our activity so we can listen more deeply to our own soul and make space for the voice of God.

Whether it's food, technology, television, work, or pleasure that keeps us distracted, over-stimulated, and entertained, a fast can open us up to God's healing presence and wisdom. You may want to consider your need to silence the eyes (from screen time), silence the ears (from incessant noise of city, radio, even talking), silence the hands (from over-working), or any other out-of-balance aspects of life that you want to ask God to help you understand and to grow in God's grace.

The silent spaces we build into our lives become the fertile ground for the wisdom of the Spirit, the word of God, and the love of Christ to dwell within us richly. We take these experiences with silence into spiritual direction and into our world to illuminate the journey.

SACRED CONVERSATION

- Underline those words or phrases in this chapter that raised questions or stood out to you as meaningful or challenging. Use those words as prompts for your journaling or prayer.
- What has been your experience with silence? If it is a regular part of your spiritual practice, how has it made a difference in your everyday life? If it is something you'd like to consider building into your practice, how do you imagine it might affect your day?
- What is your comfort level with silence? What keeps you from finding time for silence? How could you rearrange your life to provide an opening for silence daily, weekly, monthly, or yearly?
- In what areas of your life may you need to practice silence or fasting? Consider each of the areas of silencing the eyes (too much screen time), silencing the ears (too much noise), silencing the hands (too much work), silencing the lips (too much talking or eating). Which area feels most out of balance, and how can you integrate periods of silence or fasting in these facets of life?

six

The Gift of Meditation

My experience is that whether we contemplate or meditate, we should let go of formal thought or reasoning and pray at the heart-level.

—Emilie Griffin, *Doors into Prayer*

So far, the gifts we've unwrapped all have some connection with meditating on life and faith. We've meditated on our awakenings, on how we experience hospitality, and on our life story, past, present, and future. We've meditated with our journals in pilgrimage, on retreat, and in silence. Each of these gifts calls us to look deeper and consider how God speaks. Over time, meditation creates a pattern of how God speaks into our daily life, and I like to bring these messages or insights into spiritual direction to explore, confirm, or wonder *How then shall I live?*

Meditation or some form of the word is used in scripture nearly eighty-five times, depending on the translation, with a strong concentration in the Psalms. According to *Strong's Concordance*, the Hebrew word translated as *meditate (hagah)* is also translated as *ponder, imagine, murmur,* and *roar*—like a lion sinking its teeth into a meal, savoring every morsel. Meditation turns something over and over in the mind until it sinks down to feed the soul. As people seeking God in everyday life, we can ponder or meditate on most anything, but meditation isn't just an external focus of thinking about something. Rather, it takes what crosses our path and considers something more, something that speaks to the inner being, something we can welcome as a divine word for wholeness and wellness in the soul.

A REASON TO MEDITATE

The very first psalm extols the blessings and benefits that come to those who meditate on the ways of God: "They are like trees planted by streams of water, which yield their fruit in its season, and their leaves do not wither. In all that they do, they prosper" (Ps. 1:3). Strong, fruitful, life-giving, flourishing. As we receive from God, we grow, prosper, and produce fruit that will nourish first our own lives and then create an overflowing harvest to share with others.

Meditation opens our hearts and minds to the transforming ways of the Lord. For me personally, various forms of meditation have firmly planted God's word in my heart and mind, not just as a tool to remember trivial information but as a touchpoint memory of truth-telling encounters with God. That word can come not only from scripture but also from the created world around me, including people whose paths cross mine. In my relationship with my spiritual director, our conversation allows me to ponder and reflect on life, excavating the secrets of wisdom and understanding I need for this time.

Meditation is a word loosely used in today's culture to refer to anything from a silent self-emptying of the mind to quietness, peacefulness, awareness, or mindfulness. I use it in this book to mean an active and engaged opening of the heart to receive all that the Spirit wants to offer and reveal to us. One can meditate on scripture or any writing, works of art, or nature. It isn't about what we can capture and use for our own good purposes, noble as they may be. Rather meditation is the process that allows the word or image or nature to capture us and change us. It's not how we read the scripture but how the scripture reads us. It's not about the information we glean but the transformation we receive. We come to meditation with open hands, releasing all that we think we need or expect to get so that we can be free and unencumbered to receive all that God intends.

MEDITATION METHODS

Lectio Divina. This discipline of "sacred reading" from scripture speaks to everyday life in a powerful way, particularly through the Gospel stories. Choose a short passage from the Bible, and then slowly read it, listening for any word, phrase, or image that seems to resonate with meaning. Sit with that word or image in stillness for a few minutes. Then read the passage again, holding that word in your heart and listening for anything that is God-directed or Spirit-prompted. Spend time again with the word or image, perhaps beginning to journal a response to it. Ask how the

Spirit is speaking through it. Pay attention to what arises emotionally as you meditate. Is it resistance or attraction, curiosity or comfort?

The word I receive during meditation focuses my prayer and influences my interactions throughout the day. Sometimes a word or phrase stays with me for days, weeks, or even years. One phrase from the psalms that continues to rise as a prayer within me is "Give me an undivided heart" (Ps. 86:11). In my scattered, hectic, multitasking, driven mind, I need this prayer nearly every day. Another word—*dwell*—has been my constant companion that originated in my lifelong remembrance of the Twenty-third Psalm. After the line "surely goodness and mercy shall follow me all the days of my life," the psalm says, "I will *dwell* in the house of the LORD forever" (v. 6, NIV). Scripture is God-initiated dialogue. It leads us deeper into God's eternal love and faithfulness when we take time to enter the stillness and listen with heart, mind, and soul,

Visio Divina. Very similar to *lectio divina, visio divina* focuses on images rather than words. In this practice we use artwork, an icon, sculpture, movie, nature, or other forms of visual expression to attend to how God speaks to us. A specific aspect of the art or a scene in a movie may give rise to a word or impression that you want to receive as a prayer tool. How does it touch you, challenge you, move you closer to the heart of God? What do you notice in the foreground, mid-ground, background? Where do you stand in relation to each position? What are the colors, tones, or textures telling you or inviting you to consider? What question does it evoke?

I've recently begun collecting images from magazines, cards, wrapping paper, and even junk mail. When I need to change my prayer routine, I lay out all the images and words on a table and look at what captures my attention. I choose three to six images and place them on a sheet of paper or cardboard, arranging and rearranging. As I work with the images, they begin to coalesce into an expression of my heart. I am unconcerned about artistic achievement in this process. I am not trained in the arts, but I am long on experience in matters of my own heart. I know what feels right about what I'm creating and offering as prayer. Sometimes I add my own colors or doodles. After creating several collages over weeks or months, I gather them to reflect on where I've been and how I've known God in it all. It's a great way to prepare for conversation with my director.

Dreamwork. What do all the following things have in common? An emerald-green river, a boat full of people on dry land, a bonfire in the desert, a grocery cart as luggage, a race car ride down a perilous mountain. These all are symbols and images from my dreams. Although I am no dreamwork specialist, I love paying attention to my dreams and believe they are windows into the soul—unfiltered images surfacing from deep within mind and spirit.

If I remember a dream when I wake up, I record it in my journal. I write the dream in the present tense to help me stay actively engaged with it. I write about how I felt in the dream and the emotions that accompanied it. Then after I record the dream, I consider the possibilities of what the dream is telling me. I always assume that I have been given a remembered dream not to tell me about the future but rather as a gift to meditate on through journaling, art, or conversation with my spiritual director. Some people like to look at every person, symbol, and image in a dream as a part of them, representing their own life in some way.

Dreams turn into prayers when I tend to them and count them as worthy of my attention. At the end of each year, I read back through my dreams and notice patterns, both in the images that are given and in the underlying themes I discover. This anchors these messages, giving them the opportunity to continue unfolding for me even years later. They speak to me in what feels like a purer, unfiltered language of symbols brought up from the inner chamber of the heart.

Don't get me wrong, many of my remembered dreams seem like silly, crazy meanderings, as most dreams do. I can't find any rhyme or reason to these dreams, other than that they bear witness to the mystery of life that continues to speak even while I sleep. But every now and then, meditating on a dream opens new vistas.

The Prayer of Imagination. Saint Ignatius encouraged engaging the scriptures by imagining ourselves into Gospel scenes.[1] This has been an especially powerful tool for me in areas where I have felt wounded by the world. I specifically remember meditating on the story of the woman who brought an alabaster jar of perfume to anoint the feet of Jesus (see Luke 7:36-50).

In my meditation I imagined sitting at the table with Jesus. I imagined having an intimate meal with the Lord. We were enjoying each other's company when the woman with the perfume arrived. In my imagining I immediately felt defensive and wanted her to leave. After all, this was *my* intimate conversation and meal with Jesus, not hers. And when I looked at Jesus he asked, "Would you give up your seat for this woman?" This conversation with Jesus in my prayer of imagination went on for several weeks. I was angry at him for asking me this. I was also angry at the woman and confused. I obviously had some soul searching to do. Issues of faithfulness and betrayal were heavy on my mind at the time, so there was much work for me here. Ultimately it helped me come to a new awareness and deeper understanding of the ways of God's specific faithfulness to me.

Working with a spiritual director to companion us through these kinds of meditations contributes to spiritual health, keeping us balanced and focused on the path that always returns us to the truth and grace of knowing God's goodness and healing ways.

Liminal Space. Liminal space refers to the time and space between two things. It's an architectural word for those in-between functional places that get us from one destination to another in a building, be it a doorway or a hallway. But in life sometimes we get stuck in those metaphorical doorways and hallways and spend more time than necessary looking back at where we've been, looking forward to what lies ahead, or turning doorknobs of locked doors up and down the corridor. What if we stopped thinking of liminal space as transition from here to there or as a holding pattern until we get to what we perceive as the main event of life? What if we began to see the waiting as a time to breathe and regroup, observe, and behold all that life is opening or closing to us?

Liminal space also calls us to a new perspective on time. Rather than always pushing to get past the waiting for something new, we are invited to consider the gift of being in the liminal space and the time of waiting. Ancient Greeks first considered two aspects of time that seem to have importance for us in the waiting. *Chronos* is the linear passing of time, while *kairos* refers to something beyond time. Chronos asks, "What time is it? When will things change? How long, O Lord?" Kairos asks, "What is this time for? What is the purpose for this time, and am I attentive to that purpose?" Chronos quantifies time. Kairos qualifies it. Because we get antsy in what we perceive as liminal space (such as sheltering in place at home waiting for the COVID-19 pandemic to pass over us), we would be wise to shift our gaze from the clock and turn our hearts to the calling that asks, "What is this time for?"

As the wisdom of the proverb says, "Blessed, happy, prosperous . . . is the one who listens to me, watching daily at my gates, waiting at my doorposts" (Prov. 8:34, AP). Transitional gateways of life are not places to avoid or hurry from; they are places to consider, remember, honor, meditate on, and imagine what this time is for and how it may be our identifying mark of God's presence.

THE LITURGY OF DAYS

Meditation has helped me appreciate and clarify how I am called to live out my days. During my training as a spiritual director, I began to consider what my rule of life (or as I sometimes like to call it, my "liturgy of days") would look like in ordinary life. I remember the day we talked about this, a gentleman in my cohort pulled out his wallet and removed a small slip of laminated paper and said it was the rule of life he had lived by for years. I don't recall what it said, but I was taken by the idea that something like that could keep my heart and mind focused on what I truly value based on who I am.

Rules of life were developed by the early monastic communities to unify their values, calling, and faith practices. A rule of life is more than a list of disciplines, more than a reminder to pray three times a day and fast once a week. These rules were never intended as prescriptive rules or laws but rather as descriptions of ways to value and love life and draw close to God. They are simple structures aligning commitments to convictions.

To develop a rule of life, begin by assessing your relationship with various facets of life. Determine what those facets may be for you. They may include your relationships to God, self, church and ministry, family and friends, community, finances and possessions, work, technology, and home. Don't try to cover them all. Just choose three to five of the most important aspects of your life. Then work through these steps one facet at a time.

- Assess your current beliefs, conditions, and attitudes toward this aspect of life.
- How do you currently engage this facet on a daily, weekly, monthly, or less frequent basis? Does this engagement feel like it's not enough, too much, or balanced? Is it life-giving or does it feel depleting?
- What do you hope for in this facet of life? What do you most value in it? What words would describe that desire and value?

Once you've worked through these aspects (and this may take several days of meditation), summarize each one into a brief value statement and gather each statement onto one page so you can see them all together. What patterns emerge? If possible, condense or simplify your statements even further into a couple of words or a single phrase. These simple statements gain power the more condensed they become. After several weeks of working with my rule of life through prayer and the pages of my journal, I had condensed it all to five simple statements:

Dwell deeply
Journey together
Embrace story
Create hospitality
Honor silence and words

This rule becomes more of a beacon for my journey than a mission statement or a goal to be achieved. I write these words in the front of every new journal and use the rule as a template for making decisions, going through transitions, and reflecting and meditating on how I've lived out my day.

The spiritual practices I use to live into this rule of life change depending on the season I'm in. I keep these specific practices flexible and enjoy a creative combination of prayer, journaling, silence, retreats, spiritual direction, corporate worship, and scripture reading. My liturgy of days moves me from a prayer life into the unceasing life of prayer, and from there it feeds into my conversations with a spiritual director and, more importantly, becomes a gentle give-and-take of sacred conversation with the Divine.

The pathways in meditation are endless, but each path toward the loving presence of God takes me that much closer to being at home in my own life and present to my own journey, finding God with me along the way.

SACRED CONVERSATION

- Underline those words or phrases in this chapter that speak to you or open new thoughts you want to explore. Take a few minutes to be with those words and offer them as your own prayer.
- What has been your experience of meditation? How has it affected your spiritual life? How might it become part of your faith expression in the future?
- What are the liminal spaces or transitional spaces in your life right now? What does it feel like to be in this space? Spend time praying the *kairos* prayer: "What is this time for?" What happens when you receive this time as gift?
- What is your response to creating your own rule of life or liturgy of days? Does it feel like work? Or does it feel delightful? What are your areas of resistance to creating your own rule of life? How might a simple rule help orient your life and identify the things you value most?

seven

The Gift of Belonging

Prayer and solitude are ways to listen to the voice that speaks to our heart, in the center of our being. One of the most amazing things is that if you enter deeper and deeper into that place, you not only meet God, but you meet the whole world there.

—Henri J. M. Nouwen, *You Are the Beloved*

Belonging is instinctual for humanity, instilled at the beginning of time when God declared that it is not good for humans to be alone. We naturally find our places of belonging with people who become family in one way or another. As we find those welcoming places, we learn to settle into our own souls and come home to self, to God, and to living in community.

Spiritual direction is one way that I sense a coming home. Tending to the soul is tending to the Divine Spirit that dwells within. The more I can strip away my false self and get to the tender heart of true self, the more hospitable a place I create for God to dwell within me as I dwell within God. This inward dwelling or belonging ultimately leads us to an outward movement into the world.

Belonging to self and God and community is the transformation the prophet Ezekiel reports in God's promise to Israel: "I will . . . bring you into your own land . . . a new heart I will give you, and a new spirit I will put within you; and I will remove from your body the heart of stone and give you a heart of flesh" (Ezek. 36:24-26). The heart of stone represents those protective postures we take to avoid being hurt or vulnerable and that keep emotions or weaknesses under a mask of competence, power, control, shame, or victimized personas. It is ironic that all these attempts to protect the self separate us from the truth that we are created in God's image and are exactly who God intended us to be. And while our self-protective ways may separate us from our own truth, they can never separate us from God's love for us as we find our way home in our own heart-land.

COMING HOME TO SELF

You may ask, "Shouldn't I come home to God before coming home to self?" I'm not sure it matters how we define where to start because God always knows where we are. But I look to the example of Jesus' walking with the two disciples on the road to Emmaus. He joins them where they are in their discouragement—their eyes downcast—and asks, "What are you discussing with each other while you walk along?" (Luke 24:17). They share all that they had seen and heard and felt during the crucifixion of

Jesus. They acquaint themselves with their own pain and disappointment before they can even begin to lift their gaze to Jesus. Only then are their eyes open, and they know Jesus, and they know others who need to hear what they have experienced (see Luke 24:13-35).

This is of course an endless undertaking, a daily conversion of heart, mind, and spirit. Every day presents opportunities to come home to ourselves and to the love of God. An obstacle I've contended with for much of my adult life is a "not-enough" perspective in just about every aspect of life—from food, to knowledge, to possessions—always chasing after an elusive something-more to bring deeper contentment or satisfaction. Yet I claim to follow Jesus, who not only invites me to an abundant life but also says in my weakness, "My grace is sufficient." This paradox of internally wanting more while praying "I shall not want" used to bother me greatly. But somewhere along the way I was introduced to the Enneagram, which helped me explore the essence of my identity, personality, and motivations.

The Enneagram system is a tool that identifies nine different but interconnected personality types to help with unpacking motivations, distractions, perspectives, gifts, and compulsions. Like any personality tool, including the Myers-Briggs personality profile, this is simply one way to assess strengths and weaknesses as a help in discerning truths about our underlying identity. The Enneagram system is not intended to define your identity or to label yourself in a specific way but rather to open doors to exploring your true self.

Identifying my Enneagram type (I'm a 5) gave me a new perspective and awareness around many areas of tension in my life where I had spent years trying to figure out why I struggled. For instance, I believed in my heart that following Jesus offered an abundant life, yet I often responded to life with a sense of scarcity rather than abundance. I felt like there was never enough time, not enough quiet, not enough energy, not enough of me to go around. I didn't eliminate this tendency, but the Enneagram helped me become aware of it and see when this scarcity mentality is pulling me away from the all-sufficient grace of God.

I believe that the Enneagram, therapy, Ignatian exercises, and rules of life are God-given helps for learning to come home to self and come home to God. This is a great kindness that offers hospitality to self that can transform us as we encounter God and engage with others, allowing us to grow in grace and love in our relationships.

COMING HOME TO GOD

A devoted commitment to knowing God, self, and others requires what Eugene Peterson calls "a long obedience in the same direction."[1] I like this phrase because it speaks to the reality that this journey never ends and is always beginning. The eternal Christ orchestrates the evolutions of faith moment by moment and day by day. The work of the abiding Spirit within continues to construct, deconstruct, and reconstruct our lives.

What gets reconstructed within us? Just about everything—our attitudes and desires, spiritual practices, relationships, careers, the place we call home, the place we call church, and the places where we're called to bring light to the world. We exist in a constant state of change, transformation, and growth. We are always beginning again, which is why coming home to God isn't just arriving at a comfy, cozy, cuddly relationship with God. The call to abide with God comes with challenges.

The first challenge is that abiding isn't always comfortable. Deepening our roots and connections to God will call us out of our comfort zones into the deeper waters of faith lived out in the world. One who abides doesn't run away at the first hint of discord or boredom but hangs in there a little longer. I wonder how many times Jesus had the opportunity to turn away from the path set before him. The sacrifice required of him at times must have seemed too much, the band of followers he traveled with too disappointing. He could have turned his back on the whole lot but instead offered life amid trouble when he said, "In the world you face persecution. But take courage; I have conquered the world" (John 16:33). We have all that we need to abide in Christ when life gets uncomfortable.

The second challenge is that abiding is slow work. It isn't something we can measure or force along. Just as any relationship takes time to cultivate, so too our relationship with God may grow in fits and starts. As we steep tea to extract the full flavor and aroma, so too we learn to be steeped in the word of Christ until it dwells in us richly and life itself becomes a prayer, rising like incense as an aroma pleasing to God (see Colossians 3:16; 2 Corinthians 2:14-15).

The final challenge is that abiding is not limited to silence and stillness. It is easier to abide and dwell when we stop and pay attention and listen for God in a quiet surrounding, away from the hectic schedule and activity of the day. However, the example of Brother Lawrence shows us it is possible to abide within the activity of life. Lawrence was a seventeenth-century lay brother who served the Carmelite monks, and his teachings were compiled in *The Practice of the Presence of God.* He experienced the abiding presence of God in the midst of his work rather than in a monk's cell: "The time of business does not with me differ from the time of prayer, and in the noise and clatter of my kitchen, while several persons are at the same time calling for different things, I possess God in as great tranquility as if I were upon my knees at the blessed sacrament."[2]

As delightful as Brother Lawrence's experience sounds, I personally need someone to help me see that presence within my ordinary life. I'm not always immediately aware of God's presence in the moment. A regular commitment to spiritual direction continues to encourage me in this abiding with heart, mind, and spirit turned toward God. Some may see spiritual direction like a crowbar to pry us out of a bad spot or as a prod to get us unstuck so we can move on. But meeting together isn't just about figuring out life and faith in one season of life and then moving on. It's also an expression of devotion to long obedience and slow work, even when we don't perceive progress. Paying attention to the ongoing new mercies and faithfulness of God in a once-a-month meeting never gets old. This "tending the Holy" by regular habits of abiding can utterly transform life into a comfortable place to belong and dwell with God.

COMING HOME TO OTHERS

Faith Communities. Here is one thing I know for certain: Regardless of denomination, tradition, location, size, or theology, there are no perfect faith communities. If you're still on the hunt for one, stop. Don't waste any more time. They do not exist and never will until we meet God face-to-face. Once we can accept that fact, we are ready to abide deeply with and in a faith community, receiving and giving grace to one another for the journey. The offer of grace is needed precisely because our attempts to give and receive love are imperfect. In such cases, we rely on grace and forgiveness to cover a multitude of sins.

When I was looking for a new church several years ago and just couldn't find the place where I felt I belonged, I sat with my coffee one Sunday morning, borrowing lyrics from The Clash to ask God, "Should I stay or should I go?" I was tired of searching, tired of missing a faith community, and tired of coming up empty. I felt nudged to go to church, but I didn't give up my resistance. I told God, "If I go to this church, you have to give me a sign that this is where I belong if you want me to keep going." I knew I was treading close to an ultimatum here, but there was no hiding how I felt.

So I went. As soon as I crossed the threshold of that church, I was overcome with a softened heart toward the blessed gift of entering a house of worship. I can't say it was a person, the music, or the sermon—I hadn't even experienced these elements of the worship service yet. It was simply the Spirit leading me, stirring me, settling me as I sat among people I had never met, praying for a community I did not know but that would eventually become my faith community and place of belonging.

Beyond the Church. As important as a church is to me, I also experience church beyond the physical location, activities, and official programs and find Christ alive in people I meet in a variety of ways and places. This has included coworkers, writer's groups, strangers, and an eclectic small group of four women I met with for years in a monthly "listening group" as a form of group spiritual direction. I also have friends I've gathered along the way who have stayed close in my heart. We continue to connect and love one another through email, phone calls, and face-to-face visits. They too are part of my faith community.

Historical Mentors. Finally, God has gifted us with individuals through the centuries who have left a legacy of rich faith practices and wisdom for the journey. They feed my spirit when I hunger, light a torch when things are dark, or open doors to new perspectives that broaden my capacity for compassion. I see these people as my historical mentors who travel with me in spirit.

Beyond my own faith-bearing ancestors, I embrace people like Julian of Norwich, Amy Carmichael, Brother Lawrence, Annie Dillard, Richard Foster, Kathleen Norris, Eugene Peterson, and Henri Nouwen—an anchorite, a missionary, a monk, poet, pastor, and priest—and so many others. I believe God placed these people on my path to dwell with me at just the right moments to expand my faith community and inspire my growth, and I am eternally grateful.

COMING HOME TO CALLING

As we listen to God who abides within us and as we grow more deeply connected and rooted in this presence, we begin to move from the inner self out into the world. This outward movement may be surprising, especially to those who consider themselves contemplatives, but it will inevitably make itself known. As an introvert, I know that it can be easy to confuse introversion with a desire for a contemplative, quiet life of solitude. But true contemplation always leads us in God's timing out from our inner cocoon or welcomes the world into our contemplative center. It may even expand to an unquenchable desire to serve and connect with those in need in our community.

This desire often becomes a calling, something that is essential to your identity, something planted within you that God has asked you to tend. It is the deep desire that says, "I can't *not* do this." If I sit with that desire for a few days or weeks, I will know it to be a true calling if it doesn't fade away. And it will never feel contrary to Jesus' promise not to lay anything heavy or ill-fitting on me. "Walk with me and work with me—watch how I do it. Learn the unforced rhythms of grace. I won't lay anything heavy or ill-fitting on you. Keep company with me and you'll learn to live freely and lightly" (Matt. 11:28-30, The Message).

This sense of being called to service or ministry is often a slow awakening or development and requires discernment in part because we frequently get this reversed in our lives. We start out looking for purpose and meaning in outward acts of service, charity, and good deeds without first knowing the essentials of who we are in Christ. While there is not a thing wrong with serving in this way, we cannot fully find our calling through volunteering until we've claimed our own belovedness as we come home to self and to God. Then we begin to discover the gifts and calling planted within us that touch the world.

COMING HOME TO SABBATH REST

All these possibilities of coming home to God, self, and others find a mutual resting place in the practice of spiritual direction. Like gathering the harvest into the barn, so I gather all these experiences into a safe sheltered place where I lay out the facets of life to look, reflect, explore, and savor. This is a picture of sabbath rest. When we abide in spiritual direction, we stop the striving, the hurrying, and the demanding expectations, and we listen to the Holy One speaking in our own hearts.

Here we simply lay it down and acknowledge all that is stirring within the creative process of being formed as a work of art by the Creator. Sabbath rest acknowledges that the creative process involves both chaos and deconstruction, even as we experience peace and reconstruction. Sabbath is the deep sigh and silence that breathes *selah* amid the Psalms. Sabbath separates what was from what will be by pausing and making space now for what is. Sabbath receives past, present, and future as gift from the hands of our good, gracious, and generous God.

THE CALL TO BELONG

We dwell where we experience belonging. That may be our own home or someone else's home. It may be in our faith community, alone in the stillness of nature, or in the bustle of the urban landscape. If we haven't found that place of belonging in life, then we are likely on the hunt for it, driven by a longing to be at home that was placed in us at the beginning of time. Discerning this rooted identity, place of belonging, and calling in the world is the ongoing work of life and is frequently expressed in the dialogue between spiritual director and directee.

Awakening, hospitality, story, silence, pilgrimage, meditation, and belonging—these are the gifts waiting to be opened. But they all require a willingness to stretch out our hands and open our hearts to receive them as we look inside to find our own beautiful lives endowed by the image of God, kissed by Spirit-breathed purpose, and welcomed to dwell in the house of the Lord all the days of our lives.

SACRED CONVERSATION

- Underline those words or phrases in this chapter that speak to you. What attracts you to them? What questions must you consider and perspectives must you explore?
- How are you experiencing the invitations to know yourself, know God, and know others in your life? Where do you feel a need to explore more deeply?
- Who is part of your faith community? How have you experienced hurt even as you have attempted to be faithful to your community? How has your faith community been life-giving?
- What direction or longing is unfolding for you as a calling?
- What is the grace or gift you need so you can find your place of belonging and feel settled into your life?

EPILOGUE

The work of spiritual formation is never done. Always we are beginning. The fact that the landscape of the soul is always changing doesn't mean we cannot take time to stop and observe, to rest and dwell deeply together along the way.

We've unpacked and opened many gifts along our path. Don't rush off too quickly to the next thing. Take a moment to look back and consider all that has been offered and all that you have received for the journey ahead. Whether your next step is a new spiritual practice or finding a spiritual director to walk with you, I leave you with this blessing.

A BLESSING FOR THE JOURNEY

May you know the loving presence and good work of God
surrounding and guarding your heart.
May you be accompanied by "so great a cloud of witnesses" who welcome you as you are when you awaken to
the fresh mercies of God, new every morning.
May you always be an open vessel ready to receive all the
good gifts God lavishes upon you.

May these gifts continue to open into full bloom, producing rich fruit to nourish your soul, spilling over into the world around you.
May you always be at rest in your truest abiding place deep in the heart of God within you.

APPENDIX 1
A Message to Spiritual Directors

Partnering with others and listening in on their spiritual journey gives you a front-seat view of God at work in the life of another, and I rank this sacred privilege as one of the highest in all of life. It also carries a responsibility to steward and tend to the Holy within each life. New awakenings, aha moments, new freedoms, and painful awareness of loss or untended wounds all are a part of walking with others, and all are elements of the abundant life.

I offer the resources in this book to you to help open the doors of exploration to anyone who is wondering about what spiritual direction is all about. I've written directly to that person and offer these gifts as conversation starters for spiritual direction sessions. I encourage you to watch for other gifts beyond the few outlined in these chapters because the gifts of God are always surprising, abundant, lavish, and uniquely given to any who seek the Divine presence.

Here are a few ideas for using this book:

1. Encourage the directee to explore the chapters in any order, choosing a particular gift based on what resonates with the directee.
2. Encourage the directee to take their time with the material, to sit with bite-sized pieces that resonate with them and prayerfully consider where the Spirit leads.
3. You may want to encourage the directee to practice for the entire month the invitations they receive through the reading.
4. If you host day-retreats for directees, use these chapters to bring focus to your retreat time, using some of the contemplative practices and reflection questions for a given topic. (More information is provided on retreat format and options in appendix 2.)
5. Finally, you may use the material with a spiritual direction "listening group" exploring a chapter each week or month. Or select two or three chapters to offer as a test run for anyone interested in exploring spiritual direction. (Read more about listening groups in appendix 3.)

Regardless of how you choose to share this material, I pray it will enrich your life as a tool for drawing near to God's heart.

APPENDIX 2
The Seven Gifts on Retreat

Retreat is the word used in battle for soldiers to pull back, to stand down, to disengage from the front line and find refuge away from the battlefield. This is no different from the spiritual call to retreat, to step away from the grind of daily life, to unplug from the connections that continually bombard our souls.

Retreat, be it for a few hours or many days, allows us to strip away all that props us up or prods us along; it helps us carve out time and space devoted to entering the presence of God through silence, stillness, and rest. Here we tune our ears to the voice of God and sharpen our vision to the gifts around us and within us as we heed Jesus' invitation to "Come away to a deserted place all by yourselves and rest a while" (Mark 6:31, AP). The chapters of this book can be used as focal points for personal or group retreats, outlined here as half-day, full-day, or three-day retreats.

PRE-RETREAT

Arrange for your stay on retreat or prepare your place for retreat, gathering all the resources you want, including a symbol of retreat such as a candle, a small cross, or prayer beads. Determine ahead of time, which chapter you will focus on during this retreat. Prepare snacks and a thermos for coffee or tea so as not to spend a lot of time getting up and down to make another cup. A journal, a pen, and a Bible may be the only resources you need for a short retreat. For a longer stay, you may want to bring a secondary meditative reading or devotional and possibly some art supplies.

OPENING TO BODY, MIND, AND SPIRIT (1 HOUR)

Open your retreat with a three-point focus to welcome body, mind, and spirit into this time of retreat. If you plan to spend more than one day on retreat, use this exercise each morning to bring your whole self "to know the love of Christ that surpasses knowledge, so that you may be filled with all the fullness of God" (Eph. 3:19).

Body (20 minutes). Spend the first twenty minutes bringing your body into awareness that this is time for retreat. Gently stretch your hands, arms, shoulders, feet, legs, hips, neck, and back to soften muscles and relax. A few minutes of stretching and attention to your breathing will open your body to receive the care and comfort needed during this time. Concentrate on the breath of God filling your lungs and carrying oxygen to your muscles and every cell of your body. Be present and graciously welcome all of yourself to this retreat.

You may prefer simply to walk in your neighborhood, the church grounds, or retreat center. Wherever you are retreating, walk at a relaxed pace for fifteen minutes and arrive back at your retreat ready to focus. As you are bringing your body into this retreat, pay attention to anything your body may be telling you or anything that may draw you closer to God as you observe the environment on your walk.

Mind (20 minutes). Once you are back in your retreat space, take a quick inventory of your thoughts, attitudes, desires, distractions, concerns, expectations, and emotions about your retreat. After assessing what you bring with you, without commentary or judgment take fifteen to twenty minutes with your journal to freewrite all that you have observed within you. Freewriting is simply letting thoughts tumble onto the page unhindered, without pause, and without concern about handwriting, spelling, grammar, or punctuation. You may prefer to draw or sketch your inner inventory; just spend the time capturing it on the page. Allow your heart to become attentive to Christ in you.

Spirit (20 minutes). When you have worked through the body and mind exercise, reposition yourself comfortably to begin a twenty-minute Centering Prayer time (see The Gift of Silence, page 68). Some suggest sitting in a straight back chair, but it is most important to be comfortable. This time is about giving your body, mind, and spirit fully to the Divine.

Return your body, mind, and spirit to the present moment and to your surroundings. Offer a prayer of gratitude or a blessing for this first hour as you prepare to enter reflective listening. You may want to stand and stretch your arms and legs to keep the circulation moving and muscles relaxed.

REFLECTIVE LISTENING (1 HOUR)

Spend the next several minutes prayerfully reading or reviewing your selected *Sacred Conversation* chapter. Take time to pause or mark any words or phrases that tug on your heart in any way. After you've read the chapter, return to those sections that caught your attention. Reread them and choose the words or paragraph that you want to spend time reflecting on. Sit quietly with the words. Let this message move from head to heart. Then, if you desire, consider the following questions, imagining Jesus personally looking at you and listening to you:

- How do these words speak to me in this season my life? Are they words that challenge, encourage, question, comfort or call me in any way?
- What does this gift ask me to receive? What do I need to release to receive the gift more fully and completely? What is my response to receiving this gift? What is my response to releasing?
- What fears or hesitations do I notice as I unwrap this gift? How do I imagine this transaction with Jesus of receiving and releasing will play out in my life?
- What symbol might I use to memorialize this gift and this moment?

Stand and stretch or take a five-minute walk, offering prayers of gratitude.

LECTIO DIVINA (30 MINUTES)

As you listen for the prompting of the Spirit within you while you meditate on scripture, it isn't unusual to read and listen and wait but feel like you have come up empty. No word rises up from the passage. You feel no sense of prompting or calling. There is no feeling or wondering. There is just emptiness. Sometimes this is accompanied by self-doubt or a voice that says that you're not doing this right. If this is your experience, put the accusing voice aside. I have lately come to appreciate these empty spaces as invitations.

When God seems silent or distant, I receive it as a personal invitation to join in the silence and rest from all efforts to produce some insight or new perspective. Just as being with one you deeply love provides room for intimate communal silence, the silence of God is "deep calling to deep" (Ps. 42:7, AP). So, I have stopped fighting against the silence and simply let the silence give voice to my longing for God.

While reading scripture sometimes leads us to silence, it often actively engages us in conversations that lead us along the path of transformation and to a growing intimate knowledge of life with God. Use the following steps for your meditation on the Word.

1. Select a scripture passage for *lectio divina* either from a chapter in this book, verses from the Psalms, or any other passage of your choosing. Slowly and prayerfully read the passage aloud, listening for any words that resonate with you. Let those words rest in you for several minutes. This is not the time to try to study the word or cross-reference other scriptures that come to mind. Simply and quietly receive the words that capture your attention.
2. Return to the same reading and read it again slowly and prayerfully. Listen in the stillness to any prompting invitation or stirring question. Reflect on that prompting. How do you respond? What arises in you? Curiosity?

Resistance? Excitement? Gratitude? If you want, use your journal to engage in dialogue with God about these words and this prompting. Then sit quietly, letting the word of God settle within you.

3. Read the passage one last time. Listen for any further clarification or shift in your perspective on the word you are given. Receive the word again as gift and be present to it. How is the Spirit inviting you to embody this gift? How might you become this "Word made flesh"? What grace or gift of God is needed to aid you in living into this given word? Conclude your meditation and prayer with words of gratitude.

HALF-DAY RETREAT

If your retreat is only a half day, you may want to spend any remaining time, reviewing all that you have experienced during these hours. Savor the moments that stretched you, nourished you, healed you, or challenged you. Schedule time in the coming week to revisit your experiences once again as prayer and to realign where it has taken you on your journey. Unpack your experience with a spiritual director.

FULL-DAY RETREAT

If your retreat will continue to the end of the day, take time now for a lengthier break to nourish your body, take a nap, walk a labyrinth if one is available, or walk in your neighborhood if you are retreating at home. Or take on a creative experience such as photography, sketching, music, dancing, or any other outlet for your creativity. Plan on sixty to ninety minutes of focused rest-renewal time, however you best experience it.

Now slowly read through the Sacred Conversation reflection questions at the end of the selected chapter. Using your journal or notebook, write your responses to each of these questions. If you aren't accustomed to writing in a journal, you may want to jot down bullet points or just take it slow. Write your responses to one or two questions at a time and then take a break. Once you have finished, read through all that you have written and ask yourself the following questions:

- What repeated themes, words, or phrases indicate what may be important about this topic?
- What is there beyond or behind what I have written that needs to be said?
- What specific invitations to receiving and experiencing this gift am I experiencing in this season of life? How am I being invited to give this gift to others in days to come?

EXTENDED RETREAT

If you're taking a two- or three-day retreat, use the half-day and full-day outlines as your guide, and select a new chapter and explore a new gift each day. Reserve the last two hours of each day as a reflection time. Look over all that you have written, created, and considered surrounding these gifts and consider the following prompts:

- In what specific ways has this retreat renewed your body, mind, and spirit?
- What common themes connect the gifts?
- What, if anything, did God say to you or reveal to you during this retreat?
- Tell God how you feel about all that you have received.
- How do you imagine this time will follow you into your daily life in the days to come?
- What is the grace you want to ask God for as you leave your retreat setting and re-enter the world?
- What steps do you need to take when you return to live more deeply into what has been given during this time?

CLOSING BLESSING

As you conclude your retreat day, consider a symbol to take with you into the week to remind you of the gifts you have received. It can be a word written on a slip of paper, or it could be a stone, a leaf, or a shell you picked up on your walk. You may want to use a sketch you made during this time. Whatever it is, use the symbol as a reminder to fully receive and integrate the gifts into the life to which you return.

Finally, use the closing blessings at the end of the epilogue to bring closure to this time of retreat. Better yet, write your own personal blessing or prayer of thanks to the great Giver of every gift.

APPENDIX 3
A Message to the Church

Church as we know it is being recreated. This is in part due to an unexpected season of quarantine that has turned every home into our shelter, our church, and our place of community. It is in part because every digital device is now our window to the world. How these changes will affect the church in the long term remains to be seen by us. But these shifts are not a surprise to God, whose hands are around us all, forming and reforming, like the potter's hands around the clay.

Most people—churchgoers or otherwise—are noticing that these shifts have brought us into ourselves. We as a global community are being attentive to what is happening to our minds, bodies, and spirits as we have had to relinquish some faith practices that have been life-giving for years, some that have become routine habits, and some that we realize should have been released long ago. We are discerning what is important in this spiritual journey during this season of life. What is priority and life-giving? How can we experience a new closeness to the Divine while learning to be present to ourselves, to our families, and to our neighbors? This introspection, coupled with a major shift in our routines, cries for an expression of faith that is outside the realm of what has been offered by the church in the past.

Spiritual direction is one of those expressions of faith that can aid the church in partnering with its members as they explore their faith experience. Equipping the church to help people on this journey inward is the call and the heart of the gospel as Paul expressed it:

> I pray that, according to the riches of his glory, he may grant that you may be strengthened in your inner being with power through his Spirit, and that Christ may dwell in your hearts through faith, as you are being rooted and grounded in love. I pray that you may have the power to comprehend, with all the saints, what is the breadth and length and height and depth, and to know the love of Christ that surpasses knowledge, so that you may be filled with all the fullness of God. (Eph. 3:16-19)

As Paul's words illustrate, this is a triune reality of *personal revelation* in the inner being, *corporate revelation* "with all the saints," and *Spirit revelation* in the love of Christ. This prayer was reaffirmed in the fifteenth century by Thomas à Kempis who wrote, "A humble self-knowledge is a surer way to God than a search after deep learning."[1]

So how do we open the door to spiritual direction in the context of a faith community? To some degree it happens naturally as we enter relationship with the members of the church, sharing worship, prayer, and fellowship, be it face-to-face or digitally. Here we begin to know one another, to build a history together that becomes a treasure over time. We experience the spiritual gifts that are offered from each member, and this increases our vision of God at work in our midst. We "magnify the Lord" in this way to one another.

Yet so much more occurs in the inner being as we experience our life of faith. We encounter struggles, doubts, wonderings, epiphanies, and other manifestations of the Spirit at work in us, yet there is little opportunity to process these realities. I offer here ideas to open the door to the inner life experience within the faith community.

Spiritual Direction. If you have trained spiritual directors in your congregation, share that information and encourage people to take advantage of it. If your church does not have a trained spiritual director, explore the programs in your area and look for members of the congregation who have interest in becoming a director, and consider sponsoring them. Share *Sacred Conversation* with them as a first step in their exploration.

Listening Groups. This is the second way to engage the church in a form of spiritual direction, but it requires planning, specific guidance, and group norms to make it a vital resource. Most people, especially those steeped in Bible study or discussion groups, need to understand that the dynamics of a listening group are much different from that of a discussion group. The following offers a suggested approach for a listening ministry using this *Sacred Conversation* content as a guide for launching a small group.

Overview. A listening group shares the spiritual journey through contemplative practices with three to five companions. A contemplative community in small groups is the model Jesus himself set in motion first with the twelve apostles and then with the groups of three or four apostles he called for more intimate, personal connections and experiences. Weekly ninety-minute meetings over the course of eight weeks will focus on each person's faith journey as they come to know God, know self, and know others through reflection on these chapters. The Stages of Active Listening and the Group Norms that follow will help create a safe place of trust.

Format. Each week focuses on a chapter of *Sacred Conversation*; however, the first week will be an introductory session facilitated by a trained spiritual director or a ministry leader to help participants get to know one another, talk about the listening guidelines, ask questions, and share their hopes for their eight-week experience. The facilitator may continue with the group during the eight weeks or launch the group into their own listening experience with a check-in meeting after the eight weeks to discern whether the group wants to continue meeting. This is an excellent time to debrief as a group how the experience has impacted each individual. After the first week, the remaining seven weeks should follow a simple format with one member of the group facilitating to keep the group on track and watch the time of sharing so that all members have opportunity to participate.

- Opening Prayers (5 minutes)
- Check In and Topic Overview (5 minutes)
- First Look: Sharing a sentence or paragraph from the chapter that resonates with each person (30 minutes; 5 minutes per person)
- Life Together: Each person chooses one question to respond to from the Sacred Conversation section at the

end of the chapter, or they share how they experienced the gift during the week, giving an honest consideration to the challenges, surprises, and joy of where they encountered God (40 minutes; 5–10 minutes per person)

- Closing Prayer: Each person shares the grace or gift they would ask of God for the next stage of the journey (10 minutes).

Group Norms

- Keep what is said in the group confidential.
- Let others finish talking without interruption.
- Listen prayerfully on the journey together.
- Avoid cross talk and problem-solving (i.e., do not respond to what someone says with your own story or example of how you handled a similar situation).
- Maintain mutual respect among all group members.
- Be willing to let group members struggle a little as they share their challenges.
- Give room for silent pause without rushing to respond.
- Give everyone a chance to speak.
- Give each other permission to point out if the group has violated the group norms.

Stages of Active Listening

- *Receive.* Through our silent presence with one another, we remain attentive, present without distraction, tuned in and watching for the movement of the Spirit in what is being shared and what is stirring within us. We listen without moving ahead in our own inner dialogue to what we want to say next. We stay with the person speaking. We come as empty vessels to receive the words being spoken verbally, through body language, or between the lines of the conversation. We avoid trying to fix anybody's problems or offer advice about what is said. We simply hold all that is offered with a posture of welcoming grace.

- *Reflect.* Reflecting is much different from reacting to what is being said. In reflecting we stay focused on the speaker's story. If listening to the story reminds us of our own stories, triggers an emotion, or makes us want to solve a problem or persuade the speaker to think another way, we simply hold those thoughts and bookmark them in our minds to process later in our own way or with our own spiritual director.

  Reflecting as a listening tool is simply a way to mirror what someone is saying. It can take the form of repeating a phrase or a word they have used and asking if there is more they want to say about that. Reflecting may acknowledge a hurt that the individual has brushed aside as "no big deal" and holding it for them to look again. However we reflect with the individual, we do it gently, with respect, and without an agenda to persuade, dissuade, or coerce anyone to a particular conclusion or belief.
- *Respond.* If we have listened well by receiving and reflecting on what has been said, we may feel led to respond with a brief statement of what we hear or observe. Again,

> this response is not the same as reacting to what we have heard, making suggestions, or offering our own opinions. Deep listening is not the social exchange or chitchat we engage in at a church potluck or a workplace cocktail hour. Rather this is the response of holding space for the individual to breathe, the response of prayerfully listening with one ear to the speaker and one ear to the Spirit.
>
> It may be an invitation to encourage them by acknowledging strengths and gifts that you have observed in what they have shared. It may also be an opportunity to ask clarifying questions or invite the speaker to wonder about new perspectives or how they might simply live with the question or a mystery of faith for a season. How do they experience the Divine presence in their situation? What might be the invitation from God? What grace do they seek as they continue this faith journey? As we respond, we always remember that our observations, questions, and wonderings remain squarely focused on the individual, their journey, and their relationship with God.

As individuals find their way to their inner being by engaging in spiritual formation, they come to know the fullness of the living Jesus. They begin to walk the path he walked as they embrace the abundant life filled with suffering and joy, death and rebirth, dark doubts and bright resurrections. All we must do is open the door and invite them into the most incredible journey of body, mind, and spirit abiding with God, self, and others.

APPENDIX 4
Resources for Further Exploration

Following is a brief list of favorite books that I return to repeatedly as I continually begin again in my faith journey. There are hundreds of other excellent resources and writings that provide equal insight and wisdom as you continue your spiritual development. The writers I list here have been my great cloud of witnesses who surround me and offer their dialogue, points and counterpoints, and food for meditation as I find my own voice. They have opened doors and windows into my soul and have lit fires to light the way ahead. I offer space in each of these categories for you to add your own list of witnesses for your journey ahead.

SPIRITUAL DIRECTION

Bakke, Jeannette A. *Holy Invitations: Exploring Spiritual Direction.* Grand Rapids, MI: Baker, 2000.

Benner, David G. *Sacred Companions: The Gift of Spiritual Friendship and Direction.* Downers Grove, IL: InterVarsity Press, 2004.

Guenther, Margaret. *Holy Listening: The Art of Spiritual Direction.* London: Darton, Longman, and Todd, 1993.

Moon, Gary W., and David G. Benner. *Spiritual Direction and the Care of Souls: A Guide to Christian Approaches and Practices.* Downers Grove, IL: InterVarsity Press, 2004.

Nouwen, Henri J. M., Michael J. Christensen, and Rebecca J. Laird. *Spiritual Direction: Wisdom for the Long Walk of Faith.* New York: HarperOne, 2015.

Phillips, Susan S. *Candlelight: Illuminating the Art of Spiritual Direction.* Harrisburg, PA: Morehouse Publishing, 2008.

SPIRITUAL FORMATION/PRACTICES

Barry, William A., SJ. *With an Everlasting Love: Developing an Intimate Relationship with God.* New York: Paulist, 1999.

Barton, Ruth Haley. *Invitation to Retreat: The Gift and Necessity of Time Away with God.* Downers Grove, IL: IVP Books, 2018.

———. *Invitation to Solitude & Silence: Experiencing God's Transforming Presence.* Downers Grove, IL: InterVarsity Press, 2004.

Benner, David G. *Soulful Spirituality: Becoming Fully Alive and Deeply Human.* Grand Rapids, MI: Brazos Press, 2011.

Daniels, David, and Virginia Price. *The Essential Enneagram: The Definitive Personality Test Self-Discovery Guide.* San Francisco: HarperSanFrancisco, 2000.

Foster, Richard J. *Celebration of Discipline: The Path to Spiritual Growth.* San Francisco: Harper and Row, 1988.

Hagberg, Janet O., and Robert A. Guelich. *The Critical Journey: Stages in the Life of Faith.* Salem, WI: Sheffield, 1989.

Heuertz, Christopher L. *The Sacred Enneagram: Finding Your Unique Path to Spiritual Growth.* Grand Rapids, MI: Zondervan, 2017.

Mulholland, M. Robert, Jr. *Invitation to a Journey: A Road Map for Spiritual Formation.* Downers Grove, IL: InterVarsity Press, 1993.

———. *Shaped by the Word: The Power of Scripture in Spiritual Formation.* Nashville, TN: Upper Room Books, 2000.

Nouwen, Henri J. M. *Life of the Beloved: Spiritual Living in the Secular World.* New York: Crossroad, 1992.

———. *The Return of the Prodigal Son: A Meditation on Fathers, Brothers, and Sons.* New York: Doubleday, 1992.

O'Brien, Kevin, SJ. *The Ignatian Adventure: Experiencing the Spiritual Exercises of St. Ignatius in Daily Life.* Chicago: Loyola Press, 2011.

Rohr, Richard. *Falling Upward: A Spirituality for the Two Halves of Life.* San Francisco: Jossey-Bass, 2013.

Rohr, Richard, and Andreas Ebert. *The Enneagram: A Christian Perspective.* New York: Crossroad, 2001.

Thibodeaux, Mark E., SJ. *God's Voice Within: The Ignatian Way to Discover God's Will.* Chicago: Loyola Press, 2010.

PRAYER

Bourgeault, Cynthia. *Centering Prayer and Inner Awakening.* Cambridge, MA: Cowley Publications, 2004.

Foster, Richard J. *Prayer: Finding the Heart's True Home.* 10th anniversary ed. New York: HarperOne, 2002.

Keating, Thomas. *Invitation to Love: The Way of Christian Contemplation.* 20th anniversary ed. London: Continuum, 2012.

———. *Open Mind, Open Heart: The Contemplative Dimension of the Gospel.* 20th anniversary ed. London: Bloomsbury Continuum, 2019.

Laird, Martin, OSA. *Into the Silent Land: A Guide to the Christian Practice of Contemplation.* New York: Oxford University Press, 2006.

———. *An Ocean of Light: Contemplation, Transformation, and Liberation.* New York: Oxford University Press, 2019.

———. *A Sunlit Absence: Silence, Awareness, and Contemplation.* New York: Oxford University Press, 2011.

Main, John, and Laurence Freeman. *Word into Silence: A Manual for Christian Meditation.* Norwich: Canterbury Press, 2006.

APPENDIX 4

CLASSICS OF SPIRITUAL LITERATURE

These works are available electronically at ccel.org and are widely available in various translations and print formats.

Anonymous. *The Cloud of Unknowing.*

Augustine. *Confessions.*

Brother Lawrence. *The Practice of the Presence of God.*

Julian of Norwich. *Revelations of Divine Love.*

Teresa of Ávila. *The Interior Castle.*

Thomas á Kempis. *The Imitation of Christ.*

APPENDIX 5
Resources for Finding a Spiritual Director and Training in Spiritual Direction

In addition to a couple of organizations that provide more extensive directories of spiritual directors, many training organizations also provide listings of directors who have been certified through their programs. Please note this is not a comprehensive list and does not include the spiritual direction programs offered through universities and seminaries across the world.

ORGANIZATIONS WITH RESOURCES FOR FINDING SPIRITUAL DIRECTORS

- Spiritual Directors International, www.sdicompanions.org
- Grafted Life Ministries, www.graftedlife.org
- Ignatian Spirituality Center, www.ignatiancenter.org

SPIRITUAL DIRECTOR TRAINING PROGRAMS

- Christian Formation and Direction Ministries (CFDM) with regional locations and listings
  - Arizona: www.cfdmarizona.org
  - Central California: www.holeintherockministries.org
  - Nevada: www.cfdmnv.com
  - Northwest: www.cfdmnorthwest.org
  - Southern California: www.cfdmsoutherncalifornia.org
- Companioning Center, www.companioningcenter.org
- Healing Care Ministries, www.healingcare.org
- Hesychia School of Spiritual Direction, www.desertrenewal.org/hesychia-sd-school/
- Mercy Center, www.mercy-center.org/programs.html
- Pathways of Grace, www.pathwaysofgrace.com/spiritual-direction
- Schools of Sustainable Faith, www.sustainablefaith.com
- Selah Center for Spiritual Formation, www.selahspiritual.com/certificate-programs/
- Shalem Institute, www.shalem.org
- Spiritual Guidance Training Center, www.spiritualguidancetraining.com/training.html
- Stillpoint, www.stillpointca.org

NOTES

Introduction

1. Henri J. M. Nouwen, Michael J. Christensen, and Rebecca Laird, *Spiritual Formation: Following the Movements of the Spirit* (New York: HarperOne, 2010), 19.

1. The Gift of Awakening

Epigraph. John O'Donohue, *To Bless the Space Between Us: A Book of Blessings* (New York: Doubleday, 2008), 14.

1. Parker J. Palmer, *Let Your Life Speak: Listening for the Voice of Vocation* (San Francisco: Jossey-Bass, 2000), 38.
2. Saint Augustine quoted in David Benner, *The Gift of Being Yourself: The Sacred Call to Self-Discovery* (Downers Grove, IL: IVP Books, 2015), 22.

2. The Gift of Hospitality

Epigraph. Henri J. M. Nouwen, *Reaching Out: The Three Movements of the Spiritual Life* (New York: Doubleday, 1975), 72.

1. Margaret Guenther, *Holy Listening: The Art of Spiritual Direction* (Boston: Cowley Publications, 1992), 82–107.

3. The Gift of Story

Epigraph. Henri J. M. Nouwen, Michael J. Christensen, and Rebecca Laird, *Spiritual Direction: Wisdom for the Long Walk of Faith* (New York: HarperOne, 2006), 6.

1. Saint Ignatius of Loyola quoted in Kevin O'Brien, SJ, *The Ignatian Adventure: Experiencing the Spiritual Exercises of Saint Ignatius in Daily Life* (Chicago: Loyola Press, 2011), 250–51.
2. Parker J. Palmer, *Let Your Life Speak: Listening for the Voice of Vocation* (San Francisco: Jossey-Bass, 2000), 3.

4. The Gift of Pilgrimage

Epigraph. Christine Valters Paintner, *The Soul of a Pilgrim: Eight Practices for the Journey Within* (Notre Dame, IN: Sorin Books, 2015), 19.

1. Pierre Teilhard de Chardin, SJ, *The Making of a Mind: Letters from a Soldier-Priest 1914–1919* (New York: Harper and Row, 1961), 57–58.

5. The Gift of Silence

Epigraph. Martin Laird, OSA, *Into the Silent Land: A Guide to the Christian Practice of Contemplation* (New York: Oxford University Press, 2006), 2.

1. Laird, *Into the Silent Land,* 8.
2. Mary Oliver, "The Messenger," *Thirst* (Boston, MA: Beacon, 2007), 1.

6. The Gift of Meditation

Epigraph. Emilie Griffin, *Doors into Prayer: An Invitation* (Brewster, MA: Paraclete, 2001), 68.

1. Kevin O'Brien, SJ, *The Ignatian Adventure* (Chicago: Loyola Press, 2011), 141.

7. The Gift of Belonging

Epigraph. Henri J. M. Nouwen, *You Are the Beloved: Daily Meditations for Spiritual Living*, ed. Gabrielle Earnshaw (New York: Convergent, 2017), 5.

1. Eugene H. Peterson, *A Long Obedience in the Same Direction: Discipleship in an Instant Society* (Downers Grove, IL: InterVarsity Press, 2000), 17.
2. Brother Lawrence, *The Practice of the Presence of God* (Grand Rapids, MI: Spire Books, 2007), 30.

Appendix 3. A Message to the Church

1. Thomas à Kempis, *The Imitation of Christ* (Totowa, NJ: Catholic Book Publishing Corp., 1993), 20.

Recommended by
The Academy
for Spiritual Formation®
THE UPPER ROOM

For those who hunger for deep spiritual experience . . .

The Academy for Spiritual Formation® is an experience of disciplined Christian community emphasizing holistic spirituality—nurturing body, mind, and spirit. The program, a ministry of The Upper Room®, is ecumenical in nature and meant for all those who hunger for a deeper relationship with God, including both lay and clergy persons. Each Academy fosters spiritual rhythms—of study and prayer, silence and liturgy, solitude and relationship, rest and play.

With offerings of both Two-Year and Five-Day models, Academy participants rediscover Christianity's rich spiritual heritage through worship, learning, and fellowship. During the Two-Year Academy, pilgrims gather at a retreat center for five days every three months over the course of two years (a total of 40 days), and the Five-Day Academy is a modified version of the Two-Year experience, inviting pilgrims to gather for five days of spiritual learning and worship. The Academy's commitment to an authentic spirituality promotes balance, inner and outer peace, holy living and justice living—God's shalom.

Faculty trained in the wide breadth of Christian spirituality and practice provide content and guidance at each session of The Academy. Academy faculty presenters come from seminaries, monasteries, spiritual direction ministries, and pastoral ministries or other settings and are from a variety of traditions.

The Academy Recommends program seeks to highlight content that aligns with the Academy's mission to create transformative space for people to connect with God, self, others, and creation for the sake of the world.

Learn more by visiting academy.upperroom.org.